FALLING
UPWARDS

FALLING UPWARDS

Living the Dream,
One Panic Attack at a Time

JEREMY FALL

hachette
BOOKS

NEW YORK

Hachette Go, an imprint of Hachette Books
Hachette Book Group
1290 Avenue of the Americas
New York, NY 10104
HachetteGo.com
Facebook.com/HachetteGo
Instagram.com/HachetteGo

First Edition: September 2023

Published by Hachette Books, an imprint of Hachette Book Group, Inc. The Hachette Books name and logo is a trademark of the Hachette Book Group.

The Hachette Speakers Bureau provides a wide range of authors for speaking events. To find out more, go to hachettespeakersbureau.com or email HachetteSpeakers@hbgusa.com.

Hachette Go books may be purchased in bulk for business, educational, or promotional use. For information, please contact your local bookseller or Hachette Book Group Special Markets Department at special.markets@hbgusa.com.

The publisher is not responsible for websites (or their content) that are not owned by the publisher.

Print book interior design by Linda Mark.

Library of Congress Cataloging-in-Publication Data
Names: Fall, Jeremy, 1990– author.
Title: Falling upwards: living the dream, one panic attack at a time / by Jeremy Fall.
Description: First edition. | New York, NY : Hachette Go, [2023]
Identifiers: LCCN 2023001357 | ISBN 9780306830952 (hardcover) | ISBN 9780306830976 (ebook)
Subjects: LCSH: Fall, Jeremy, 1990– | Restaurateurs—United States—Biography. | Businesspeople—United States—Biography.
Classification: LCC TX910.5.F35 A3 2023 | DDC 647.95092—dc23/eng/20230310
LC record available at https://lccn.loc.gov/2023001357

ISBNs: 978-0-306-83095-2 (hardcover); 978-0-306-83097-6 (ebook)

Printed in the United States of America

LSC-C

Printing 1, 2023

To the outliers, the others, the weird kids, the ones with bad credit, the ones that were made fun of for being different. To the liars that felt like they needed to bullshit to fit in—you beautiful motherfuckers, this is for you.

Contents

FALLING
UPWARDS

1

THE BRUNCH

Or, the Panic Attack That Saved My Life

IN FEBRUARY 2019, I WAS STOKED TO BE INVITED TO JAY-Z'S ROC NATION GRAMMY party, an exclusive Hollywood event otherwise known as "The Brunch." I spent some time thinking about what to wear, before settling on a more formal version of my usual sweatpants and T-shirt attire. A designer loaned me an all-black silk jogging suit, which was both exciting and practical, because an elastic waistband would be vital for this Brunch—I was, as usual, hungry AF, and my goal was to be King Bloat at that black truffle pasta bar.

The cavernous, white party tent was filled with elegant chandeliers, constructed from thousands of roses, peonies, and birds of paradise. It looked like an English country garden in there; they'd gone all out, for sure. But something about all the flowers took me back to a year ago, Jared's memorial, his smiling face in a large, framed photo surrounded by wreaths, flowers, and messages from loved ones.

Jared was my friend, a mentor who helped me launch my career in Hollywood. He had gotten his start managing a bar for a friend in Reno, where he found himself at the heart of the cocktail culture explosion and invented his own take on a Royal Fizz using Auchentoshan Scotch, malted milk, Art in the Age Root, house-made sassafras bitters, and one whole egg, topped with house-brewed sarsaparilla and atomized cinnamon tincture—a daunting list of ingredients that added up to a grown-up root beer float.

I met him in 2014 at the opening of Harlowe, a bar and restaurant in West Hollywood, after I'd DMed the Harlowe Instagram account a week before the opening party to say congrats. Jared had responded, saying he'd be glad to put me on the list, and that he'd heard of me.

I was only twenty-three but already had eight years of Hollywood nightlife under my belt, starting at age sixteen when I found myself running the door at celebrity hot spot Les Deux, and going on to have my own club nights at the Avalon in Hollywood during the short-lived but spectacular Hollywood club scene of the 2000s.

It was a high-energy, decadent time to be a kid in LA, and I found myself at the heart of a nonstop party, becoming one of the first promoters to bring DJs from the Paris scene to LA, booking Justice and other French acts for dirt cheap, and even hosting a secret show by an upcoming artist, Lady Gaga. The electroclash dance genre had emerged in the clubs of Munich, New York, and Paris and made its way to LA in the early 2000s, combining new-wave aesthetics with a synth-pop, techno, and punk sound, all rolled up in the DIY drama of performance art. It was trashy, underground, decadent, and above all, fun. Artists like Peaches, Ladytron, Fischerspooner, and Scissor

Sisters provided the soundtrack for the first "hipsters" to dance to. The Hollywood electroclash scene was filled with kids who had been raised on punk and rave, and you'd often see members of the Rapture and the Yeah Yeah Yeahs partying alongside everyone else. It was an innocent and irreverent time, pre-iPhone, pre-fentanyl, and pre-recession. Rents were cheap in LA—you could rent a bungalow in Hollywood with your friends for $750 a month—and at night, up and down Hollywood Boulevard, clubs and bars were erupting with young Myspace stars, starlets, and emo kids dancing side by side to electroclash anthems like "Fuck the Pain Away."

This was all very much within my creative wheelhouse—and if there was one thing I'd been raised to understand, it was customer service. I started working at my mom's café in Downtown LA when I was eleven, so actually, I had a good thirteen years in hospitality under my belt by the time Jared gave me the opportunity to open my own spot. I may have been young in years, but I had earned enough stripes for someone as experienced and respected as Jared to give me the time of day.

At the Harlowe opening party, I made a beeline for Jared and introduced myself. Immediately, there was a rapport, a sense of a shared mission. Electroclash was over, having fizzled out almost as quickly as it exploded onto the scene, and Hollywood's thriving homegrown indie nightlife scene was morphing into something soulless, commercial, and focused on false notions of "VIP," whatever the fuck that meant. Jared, like me, was frustrated and embarrassed, even, at how cheesy Hollywood nightlife had become. The douchey bouncers, the long lines, the exorbitant cover charges—it was a shit show, and it felt like everything cool had been sucked out of my town overnight.

Jared was ten years older, but I think he saw a little of himself in me. I was hungry for success and had been for years. My mind was always in a state of pathological activity, turning constantly with ideas and concepts, to the point that some nights, I couldn't even sleep because of the never-ending train of thoughts and concepts. I didn't know then what I know now—that I'd been carrying around an undiagnosed anxiety disorder for years—but it didn't matter at the time. The anxiety was what made me jump out of bed in the morning and get to work.

I think Jared found my passion endearing, to some degree. I was just a kid, and he knew the ropes, but it was obvious that we were both rule-breakers, cut from the same cloth, which made it easy for me to share my vision with him.

"I want to re-democratize LA nightlife," I said. "Have it feel lawless again, make it unique. Like it used to be, in the 2000s, or like Studio 54 in the 1970s."

Studio 54 is when American nightlife peaked, in my opinion, and I was obsessed. I'd watch documentaries about that era, over and over. I read *Party Monster* at least once a month, trying to channel the energy of New York Club Kid life. I'd never experienced it myself, but my father had. He grew up in New York, and in his twenties he bartended at Mr. Chow's and would frequent Studio 54, Palladium, and Limelight, back when nightclubs were glamorous and exciting because they were populated by creatives who came out of an underground culture.

"That's what I want for Hollywood," I told Jared. "Places like that. Nightclubs that are breeding grounds for ideas and friendships and art."

He seemed interested in what I had to say, so I kept talking.

"Look, everyone's doing the same shit," I said. "Craft cocktails, Edison bulbs, and Foster the People on one side of the spectrum, bottle service and Lil Wayne on the other. Nothing in between. And menus, there's such a fucking formula, you know? Kale salad, hamachi crudo, beef cheek, pork belly, always a poutine, I mean come on!"

I was fully ranting now.

"Also, enough mixology, PLEASE."

His eyebrows rose—Jared was Mr. Mixology, and here I was, this little asshole, trying to school him at the opening of his own bar? Again, he was gracious enough to humor me.

"So what's wrong with mixology, Jeremy?" he asked, seemingly genuinely interested in what I might have to say. Which was a lot.

"Every bar is the same. Cocktails in Mason jars. Five hundred different kinds of Old Fashioned: Walnut Old Fashioneds, Maple Syrup Old Fashioneds, Bacon Old Fashioneds. Aperol spritzes, St. Germain. And Fernet. God, Fernet tastes like ass. It's all part of the same recipe. I fucking hate recipes. Recipes are ceilings, rules, limits, guidelines, telling us how we need to do things. What the right way is. And we need to get rid of them."

"Well, what are you going to do about it?" Jared asked.

"Something different."

"Can you be more specific?"

"We need a new template. Like, a mini dance club, with no bullshit cover, no douchey bouncers, no attitude. A simple email RSVP will suffice. No dress code. No self-conscious 'see and be seen,' 'beautiful people' West Hollywood bullshit. People need to feel welcome when they walk in, like they're part of a family that will accept them exactly how they are. Maximum capacity eighty people, all of them special, from all walks of life. Famous people, sure, they can come if they want, but they're going to stand in line with everyone else. And no fucking mixology, no seventeen ingredients—everyone drinks simple cocktails based on great ingredients. Then we let loose. Big time."

Jared nodded, absorbing my diatribe.

"So . . . I think you're saying you want to open a bar?" he said.

"Yeah," I said. In truth, I hadn't really thought about it. But yeah, now that he came to mention it, I did.

"You know, we have this attic above Sassafras that's unused," Jared said. "How about a pop-up? Think you can handle it?"

Sassafras was a gorgeously baroque Southern-themed bar on Vine Street in the heart of Hollywood. Having a pop-up bar on the premises meant I wouldn't have to worry about getting a liquor license. All I'd have to worry about was being creative as fuck, and packing the place.

Suddenly, I felt butterflies in my stomach. This was one of those fork-in-the-road moments. The kind you look back on, the chance encounters that change your life, the random conversations that unexpectedly transport you from kid to adult.

"What do you think, Jeremy?"

Before I could respond, I started coughing—I always coughed when I got nervous, and it was annoying as hell. Convulsing and spluttering, I managed to get the words out.

"Yeah, man, let's do this!"

This conversation happened in January 2014, and by July, Genesis, my nightlife concept above Sassafras, was open, starting as a pop-up every Saturday night. I had my first bar in Los Angeles, at the age of twenty-three. The name alluded to new beginnings—yes, I was trying to reinvent partying and take it back to its roots, but I was also trying to reinvent myself and find a place where my creativity could shine, where I could design an entire space and experience, and curate every aspect of it. I felt ready, but it could never have happened without someone experienced, like Jared, vouching for me, backing my vision, and understanding exactly what I was trying to do.

To get into Genesis all you had to do was email an RSVP to RSVP@ wtfisgenesis.com. As promised, there was no cover, no guest list, no promoters, no craft cocktails, no snobbery, no red carpets. Just pure, unadulterated liberation. Recipes out the fucking window. Genesis was the beginning of me, my anti-Hollywood love letter to Hollywood, a new manifesto for nightlife, in my eyes.

Jared's PR team told all the nightlife blogs what we were doing, and a ton of journalists RSVPed, curious to see what I was up to. A non-douchey club night in Hollywood? A fuck you to VIP culture? Cool! They may not have known who I was, but they were all about the narrative.

"Jeremy Fall, the young LA nightlifer, wants to change the way we go out. Are we ready for it?" *Time Out* asked.

On opening night, Jared and I were stunned to see lines around the block. In the alcove filled with taxidermy and antiques, we watched as people raised their hands in the air like it was church. Seems like I hadn't been the only one itching to change things up and reclaim a little bit of that outlaw spirit. The Genesis concept was a hit, and before long, my little pop-up became a permanent fixture.

At that point, it was a no-brainer when I asked Jared to back me as I launched my second project that same year. Golden Box was Genesis on steroids, in the old Writer's Room, behind Supper Club on Hollywood Boulevard. In there I created an unabashedly on-the-nose tribute to Studio 54, filling the place with golden disco balls and lining the floors with vintage covers of Andy Warhol's *Interview* magazine. The walls were paint-splattered and DJs spun from inside a golden cage. I made sure there were very few places to sit because this was a place to dance. To lose yourself in the dark, without worrying about who was watching you. The capacity was two hundred and once again there was

NO mixology, NO cover charges, NO sleaze, NO multilevel warehouse bullshit. Just a room where magic happened at night, and once again, the media was all about it.

"Want to hear more about Fall's plan to conquer LA nightlife? Read our interview with him here!"

Now, it was official—I was a thing. A "Nightlife Person." I felt a little odd, thinking of myself that way. Something about it didn't feel quite "me." But I wasn't about to nitpick—if people wanted me to be the Nightlife Guy, sure. The customer is always right. Jared took pride in me, his six-foot-seven protégé, and based on the success of Genesis and Golden Box, we decided to partner up a third time, when we relaunched the infamous King Eddy Saloon in Downtown, the oldest speakeasy in the US.

The King Eddy was, how can I put it, a whole different vibe. Notorious in Los Angeles, it was widely known as maybe the sleaziest, gnarliest dive in Downtown, open at 6 a.m. to serve a hardcore clientele consisting of Skid Row's down and out, and hard-partying hipster kids.

The King Eddy was just blocks from where I grew up with my mom, and I didn't tell Jared this, but it was a little emotional for me, coming back to this part of town. My memories of the place were not especially happy. We were broke, not homeless by any means, but financially insecure, living paycheck to paycheck amid the maelstrom of deprivation and addiction on our doorstep. As a child, the memories of the lost souls I encountered in the streets of DTLA—hunched over, nodding out, hopeless—became imprinted on my psyche.

I thought by going back there, and working on a bar with Jared, I might be able to reframe my relationship with Downtown, but the energy was off this time. Jared seemed increasingly on edge these days. And Downtown wasn't that happy to have me back—I was Mr. Hollywood now, and one night someone graffitied RIP JEREMY FALL on a wall at the King Eddy. It was starting to feel like a bad idea.

Shortly after we opened, two members of our staff died by suicide in close succession—a tragic, unnerving sequence of events that, for me, signified the end of the magic carpet ride. I felt the overwhelming need to escape nightlife and the dark, sad, alcoholic elements underpinning it. I eased out of the world Jared and I had inhabited as a team, and I knew he wasn't coming with me—he was a Nightlife Guy through and through.

"What are you going to do with yourself now?" he asked, when I told him I was exploring new pastures.

"I want to go back to my roots," I said. "It has to be food."

"Food? But you don't have any experience in the food industry. No one's going to take you seriously."

"I have a little experience," I said. "I think it'll be good."

Growing up above the café my mother managed on Skid Row, I'd always found comfort in the rituals of food. Simple comfort food, done well. And if there was one thing my anxious mind was craving at that moment in time, it was comfort. But like everything, I wanted it to be different, revolutionary, somehow. I got lucky—the club where I'd run the door, Les Deux, had been revamped with a restaurant spot in the back, so I pitched the owners a pop-up concept, much like I had with Jared, except this would be a nightlife-meets-dining concept. Breakfast in the middle of the evening, with cereal-themed cocktails. Diners would get a newspaper and a cup of coffee upon arrival, and then they'd choose from a breakfast-heavy menu of drunken challah French toast or "Benedict" fries with raclette cheese and smoked paprika hollandaise. I decided to call it Nighthawk, after Edward Hopper's 1942 painting *Nighthawks*, depicting an all-night diner with three customers, all lost in their own thoughts.

Again, my youthful enthusiasm won everyone over, and the owners of the space agreed to give me a shot. I convinced Chef Greg Schroeppel from Spago in Beverly Hills to run the kitchen. My bartender, Giovanni Martinez, would serve "spiked cereal milk" cocktails and boozy floats to pair with the breakfast-at-midnight fare, and music would come via a live DJ "jukebox" where diners could request their tunes directly. All this from 10 p.m. to 2 a.m. on Fridays and Saturdays only, at first.

The owners wanted to test things out, see how people would react. This was my first venture without Jared by my side, and everyone was anxious to see how it would be received. That hacking, nervous cough of mine was nonstop in the weeks leading up to our January 2016 opening on Las Palmas Avenue in the heart of Hollywood.

I'm pleased to say, the gamble worked. Honestly, I probably wouldn't be writing this book if it hadn't. Nighthawk became my megahit and changed the course of my life. The anxiety-fueled mania that had always caused me to give birth to contrary, random, upside-down ideas was proving to be my greatest ally, as was my ability to "paper-clip" separate concepts together—cereal + booze, breakfast + dinner, nightclub + bar, etc. Paper-clipping was becoming my trademark, the key mechanism behind the explosion of Jeremy Fall, the brand.

"Money, success, it's all smoke and mirrors," my dad told me once, explaining the success of Studio 54, and now I could see he was right. Sometimes you do have to be a little mad, a little manic, to dream this hard. To imagine worlds that make no sense until you build them, yourself, brick by brick, and have the guts to share them.

Before long, my bank balance indicated that I wasn't broke any-more. I wasn't sleeping on friends' floors, or crashing in a buddy's closet like I had while promoting clubs in Hollywood. It was surreal when Jay-Z's management company, Roc Nation, said they wanted to sign me and make me the first Food Guy on their roster. From Red Carpet Guy to Bar Guy to Food Guy, all by the age of twenty-three. I couldn't believe how rapidly life was moving, and this new world of financial stability and "success" didn't even feel real to me. Most days, I felt like an imposter in my own dream.

Jared was the biggest dreamer I knew, next to me. He had imagined and built many worlds from scratch, injecting heartbeats into empty cubes all over Hollywood. But there was something inside, something slowly consuming him, decimating the part of him that wanted to live. Call it addiction, call it mental illness, or just the occupational haz-ards of working in nightlife . . . who knows what it was. He was only thirty-eight when something finally overshadowed his will to live, with a self-inflicted gunshot to the head in a small cottage in Echo Park, Los Angeles. That was how his story ended, in 2018. It was unimag-inable, to me, how his bright star could have imploded so quickly, how his dreams could have slid into nightmares.

One year after his death, as I walked through the beautiful, flower-bedecked brunch party in Beverly Hills, I wished Jared could have been there with me. My journey from being a broke kid on Skid Row to this party was thanks to him, my fairy godfather, telling me he believed in me and my wild, loose balloon ideas. It was making me feel sad, thinking about it, and when I feel sad, one thing always helps. Food.

I walked over to the pasta bar and loaded my plate with black truf-fle cavatappi, inhaling the creamy, decadent aromas. Some people don't eat at these parties, but I will never, ever say no to black truffle pasta, because that shit is fire. Also, I'm the Food Guy, therefore my plate should never be empty. That would be rude.

Looking for a table, I walked past Jay-Z, Usher, and Kevin Hart having a conversation about Black excellence and thought about sixteen-year-old Jeremy—he would be so hyped to see himself now, age twenty-nine, at a party with icons, my name in *Forbes* magazine's "30 Under 30" issue. I had legitimately checked all of my sixteen-year-old self's boxes, and in theory, I should have been feeling on top of the world.

But there it was again. The Cough. Unlike everyone else at The Brunch, my anxiety cough didn't need an invitation, and it always loved to show up at the worst possible moment. I tried to suppress the hacking, but it wasn't working. I knew it probably wouldn't stop for at least an hour, so I had to make a decision. With nowhere near enough pasta in my belly, I decided to bounce.

I said a few quick goodbyes on my way out, making sure not one of those people knew what was really going on—that I was about to have a full-blown anxiety attack. I was used to this shit by now, and had always been good at keeping my little issue to myself, except, it wasn't a little issue anymore. I was anxious all the time.

About a red light.

A green light.

About being two minutes late, about how people would react to me.

About an elevator door—what if someone was standing on the other side when it opened? What would I do? Would I go out first? Would they come in?

The quick-fire, hyper-aware thoughts that had once fueled my imagination were beginning to run out of space in my head.

Outside the party, I got in the shuttle that took people to their cars, and the driver looked at me.

"Already leaving, man?"

"Yep."

I stayed quiet the rest of the ride to my car, my heart racing, coughing into my sleeve, droplets of sweat on my brow. I had this under control.

My MOM TOLD me that when I was a kid, it would take me forever to get up steps. I would put one foot on one stair, the other foot on the same stair, then wait a minute as I summoned the courage to tackle the next step. Twenty minutes total to climb four steps, and kids would run around me, laughing, calling me wuss, scaredy-cat, and when I was older, "fag."

Being called names made me angry for a long time, and the way I coped was by working. My career was a shield against criticism, a "fuck you" to a world that insisted my masculinity should look a certain way, that bullied little boys who took twenty minutes to go up the stairs because they never believed the ground could be solid beneath them since they'd grown up broke. *Go full force into your career, Jeremy.* That was my thinking for fifteen years, and mental health never entered into the picture. Why would it? I was succeeding—so what if I was a little manic, a little stressed out? So what if I coughed like I had a fucking disease?

The cough had started in 2014, same year I met Jared. Same year I opened Genesis. He and I would be mid-conversation, and I'd have to step out of the room because the coughing was triggering my asthma, and I wouldn't be able to breathe. Then I'd have to get a ride to the hospital, because I didn't have insurance, and who the fuck can afford an ambulance? Jared knew what it was like, being so busy with work you forget to look after your health, so he told me, "Don't let little issues snowball into big ones, Jeremy."

I knew he was right, so I got the cheapest insurance I could find and went to a doctor. Then another. And another. Six different doctors, none of whom could figure out what was going on with me. One of them gave me an endoscopy; he said the cough was corroding the insides of my chest and stomach, and he put me on a diet of white chicken with no salt. For someone who is absolutely obsessed with food and will literally consume ten pounds of McDonald's to himself, bland chicken is a prison sentence. By the way, here's what ten pounds of McDonald's looks like: two Big Macs with extra cheese, two cheeseburgers, a lot of chicken nuggets, a lot of fries.

Doctor Number Seven finally figured out what was going on.

"Your cough is triggered by psychiatric illness. People with anxiety disorder are prone to poor breathing habits and hyperventilation, during which it can feel as though your throat is closing, and that's what's causing you to cough." That was the first time I ever heard the term "anxiety disorder." Apparently I had "somatic cough syndrome," or a "psychogenic cough," and it seemed like until I figured out the anxiety shit, I would just have to deal.

Millennials. We're busy people. Born somewhere between the fall of the Berlin Wall and the creation of nip slips, we've been overprescribed Ritalin for our ADHD; we got Botox at twenty-two while worrying about climate change, the opioid crisis, school shootings, pandemics, domestic terrorism, and the collapse of the world system, in general. Still, I felt like I was doing okay, compared to most people in the world. I was one of the lucky ones. I had turned my disadvantage into privilege. I was sure I could handle a dumb cough by myself, and not let it affect my life any further.

Or could I?

Can we lead with authority and strength when we feel anxious? Can we inspire and motivate others when our minds and hearts are racing? If we suppress the anxiety in an attempt to appear in control, where do those feelings go? Psychologist Rollo May first wrote in 1977, "We are no longer prey to tigers and mastodons, but to damage to our self-esteem, ostracism by our group, or the threat of losing out in the competitive struggle. The form of anxiety has changed, but the experience remains relatively the same." Meaning, even though we're not being chased by T. Rex, we are nonetheless still subject to the debilitating effects of uncertainty, and those worries still provoke the same neurological and physical responses felt by cave people at the sight of a saber-toothed tiger.

According to the Anxiety and Depression Association of America, "Stress is a response to a threat in a situation. Anxiety is a reaction to the stress." Anxiety is fear of what might happen in the future. Sometimes that fear is rational. Sometimes not. Sometimes it's about something that will happen in three minutes or in thirty years. Anxiety is everywhere, and in the United States, anxiety is the most prevalent mental disorder, with data from the National Institute of Mental Health indicating that about 30 percent of Americans experience clinical anxiety at some point in their lives. Anxious people react quickly in the face of danger. We are more comfortable with uncomfortable feelings, because hello—welcome to my life. We can be more resourceful, productive, and creative, and our tendency to worry can break down barriers and forge bonds between us and nonanxious people, because who else is going to text you to make sure you got home, took your vitamins, or ate your kale?

But left unchecked, anxiety distracts us, kills our energy, and drives us to make poor decisions. Anxiety can be a powerful enemy, and if we don't look our anxiety in the face at some point, it will eventually take us down. They say the first step is to identify your anxiety: how it manifests itself and how it feels. Then you can take action to manage it, day-to-day and in challenging moments, so you make smart decisions that aren't born of fear. And the final enemy of anxiety is a strong support infrastructure. A way to share what you're going through. Once you learn to accept and manage your anxiety over the long term, you'll start succeeding not in spite of your emotions, but because of them.

All of this is much easier said than done, of course, especially when, like me, you're in no mood to even take the first step, because you're just too busy being anxious.

THE SHUTTLE ARRIVED at the parking lot where I had left my car. On my passenger seat was my copy of the *Forbes* "30 Under 30" issue. When I had posted the news to my Instagram, my caption was "look ma, no hands." Her son, the little asshole who shot BB guns at cars on Melrose and sold Pokémon cards so he could afford to buy sodas from the vending machine at school, had "made it." Being in *Forbes* told me that everything was going to be okay, that Mom and I weren't going to be broke anymore, and I'd never have to hear the mad screams of someone shooting speedballs outside my bedroom window, terrified because they were so high they couldn't see. Nope. That was never going to be my life again.

I pulled onto Sunset Boulevard and drove its long, winding curves too fast. I often drove dangerously fast when I was anxious, probably because I wanted to be anywhere but where I was. Having a mind that can't keep up with itself means you have all this excess energy, and it has to go somewhere. For me, it went into eating and breaking speed limits. This was definitely one of the more hazardous aspects of my anxiety—it turned me into a classic asshole LA driver, a speed freak.

The light in front of me turned red and I came to an abrupt halt. The driver next to me rolled down their window and yelled, "You on drugs? Slow down!"

No, I wasn't on drugs, and maybe that was the problem, according to some of my friends and my doctor. They said I should look into anti-anxiety medication, anti-depressants, but there was no fucking way I was putting that shit in my body. That had been my bottom line, forever. I'd heard medication can dull you, take away your fire, and I had worked too damn hard to risk numbing myself into mediocrity, and limiting the creativity that was the heart and soul of who I was in the world.

I pulled over. It was hard for me to focus on the road, and I felt like I might get into an accident. I didn't want that. I wanted to live. I wanted to enjoy life. Things were supposed to be good, the best ever, and I didn't understand why I was feeling like this. I needed to talk to someone, but I wasn't sure who, so I called my publicist and tried to sound casual.

"Hi!" I said, too brightly.

"Oh, hey, Jeremy! Congrats on *Forbes*, the issue looks great!"

I glanced at the magazine on the passenger seat again. Life was going exactly to plan. Wasn't it?

"Aren't you supposed to be at The Brunch?" she said.

"Yeah. I just left."

Suddenly, I had an idea—ideas often came to me when my mind was spun out like that. Ideas that stretch the boundaries of workability, but were worth having anyway, because thinking abstractly and laterally are the keys to creative innovation. Loose balloons: the best, craziest ideas ever, concepts that will never work but that keep me excited. Loose balloons come from the maddest and most random corners of your creativity. Loose balloons lead you to places of true innovation, like Brian Jones's Moroccan album or Lou Reed's *Metal Machine Music*. Loose balloons are weird AF, and I love 'em, which is why I have one tattooed on my left arm.

"Hey, what if I open a restaurant where the menu is curated every night, not by the chef, but by the customers?" I said. "The customers write the menu? Every night?"

"Yeah! Like, an amazing, collaborative dinner party. That's so interesting."

"I mean, obviously, it would be impossible to apply that idea in a disciplined way that would allow us to have a sustainable and healthy business, and it would probably close after a week. But kinda dope, right?"

"The press would go nuts."

"Yeah, it's impossible though. Gotta go."

I hung up. There was still no way I could drive, feeling like this. How could I ever get home?

I wished I'd told my publicist how I was really feeling. But I didn't know how to show her that part of myself. Scared, vulnerable, anxious, spiraling Jeremy didn't pair well with the image I had spent so many years crafting. I was supposed to be large and in charge, always in control. If she realized I wasn't, maybe she'd start pressuring me to get medicated too. Then I wouldn't have my loose balloons. Then I'd stop having wild ideas that I could paper-clip together into a legacy. Without my crazy, I'd be nothing.

Depression feels like nothing. An inexplicable lack. No excitement, no anger, no pain, no love, no attraction, no sadness. Hiding behind a shield of bullshit so deep that you don't even remember how to climb out of it. No strength or courage to piece the puzzle back together and pull out of it before your whole world slowly bursts into flames. That was my greatest fear.

For years, I'd been chasing dreams in order to feel validated. Boxes on a checklist were my currency for happiness, and in escaping my fear of Nothingness I was now stuck, racing up an infinite ladder towards . . . This. Me on the side of Sunset Boulevard with my hazards blinking, no idea where the fuck I was going, or why.

I had tried deep breathing exercises. I knew it activated the para-sympathetic nervous system and created an immediate soothing mech-anism. I knew about moving my body, getting my heart rate up with a walk, stimulating the release of dopamine, serotonin, and noradren-aline in your brain. I knew about meditation, how it was supposed to give our brains a soothing neurochemical bubble bath. None of that had worked for me.

Then I felt it again. The sense that this was a moment in time. One that would change me, and push me towards a better version of myself, closer to the *real* journey, maybe one where I didn't have to feel so alone in this mind of mine. I couldn't save Jared—maybe no one could have—but maybe I could save myself. It was time to let my anxiety go, and just trust that wherever I landed, it would be somewhere better than this.

2

THE PAPER CLIP MENTALITY

My Paradigm for Creating Cool Shit

EOPLE HAD BEEN TELLING ME "YOU NEED TO GO INTO THERAPY" FOR YEARS, AND my stock response was always to laugh.

"So I'm a little loopy. You should love me just the way I am."

I never took it seriously. Not until that Grammys brunch, that meltdown on the side of Sunset Boulevard when I started to suspect that maybe, probably, my friends had a point. Something wasn't working right in my head. Maybe I couldn't fix it myself. Maybe it wouldn't just go away by itself.

It was easy for me to find a thousand reasons not to seek help. I didn't know how to get therapy, or what the first steps even looked like. They don't teach you this stuff in school. They just tell you to Google the Suicide Prevention number, and good luck.

A few months later, I found myself in the throes of yet another public anxiety attack, in the parking lot of Sugarfish in West LA, one of my favorite restaurants—the sashimi is the shit. There I was, waiting for my order, spiraling like a motherfucker for no apparent reason. This was definitely going to get in the way of me enjoying my lunch, and that's when it occurred to me that maybe I should actually get some help. All that good toro going down the drain was outrageous. I didn't want this happening to me ever again.

I thought about the people in my life who I could maybe talk to about this, and all of them were women. Interesting. Dudes, we don't talk about this stuff a lot. At least, we didn't back then.

I called my girl Firam, a musician, who had spoken publicly about her own struggles with mental health.

"Firam, I think I need therapy, what do I do?"

"First, that's a really great thing to do for yourself."

"Thank you. Yeah, and I think I need a woman therapist, not a dude. I prefer talking to women about this stuff. So yeah, someone who gets it. Someone who feels like a friend."

"Look, it's hard to find a good therapist," Firam said. "It's kind of like dating. Usually, you have to shop around a little bit, sometimes it takes a minute before you find the right one. So you gotta be patient. But I think I have someone who might work for you. Some good friends of mine speak very highly of her."

"Who is she?"

"Her name's Sarah. I'll get her number and text it to you. Okay?"

Minutes later, she texted me Sarah the therapist's number, and I booked my first session with her straightaway. As soon as I received confirmation of my appointment the following week, I felt calmer. There was something empowering about taking action, even though

I still had major concerns about the whole therapy business. Things I would have to bring up with Sarah when we spoke.

I needed to be sure I was doing the right thing for myself, for my business, and for my future as a creative person. Therapy might work for a lot of people, but aren't all the greatest artists, business visionaries, and creatives a little . . . out there? Is mental stability really necessary when you're trying to smash paradigms and think outside the box? Mental illness seemed like a common denominator when it came to creativity, historically, so why was I about to get rid of mine?

Celebrated Norwegian artist Edvard Munch's life was fraught with anxiety—his masterpiece, *The Scream*, came to him in a dark vision as he stood on the edges of Oslofjord. "The sun began to set—suddenly the sky turned blood red," he wrote. "I stood there trembling with anxiety—and I sensed an endless scream passing through nature." The painting is thought to represent the angst of modern man, which Munch experienced throughout his life, but saw as a driver of his art. "My fear of life is necessary to me, as is my illness. They are indistinguishable from me, and their destruction would destroy my art."

Here's what Vincent Van Gogh wrote in a letter to his brother Theo in 1888: "I am unable to describe exactly what is the matter with me. Now and then there are horrible fits of anxiety, apparently without cause, or otherwise a feeling of emptiness and fatigue in the head . . . at times I have attacks of melancholy and of atrocious remorse."

People working in creative fields, including dancers, photographers, and authors, are 8 percent more likely to live with bipolar disorder. Writers are 121 percent more likely to suffer from the condition and nearly 50 percent more likely to commit suicide than the general population. Keep an eye on your writer friends, everyone.

Psychologists have established a link between mental illness and creativity, but they are still piecing together the mechanisms that underlie it. Studies appear to suggest that the key to creative cognition involves opening the floodgates and letting in as much information as possible, because the most bizarre associations can turn into the most productively creative ideas. But the problem with having a million thoughts and ideas floating around your head at any given moment is that it can, as we've seen, make you lose the will to live.

Here's the first thing I said to Sarah, who I now call my Sarahpist.

"Look, I want to try therapy so I can stop my thoughts spiraling all the time, but I do NOT want medication, okay? Bottom line."

"Sure, Jeremy," she said. "You're steering the ship."

"How does that shit work, anyway? Just out of curiosity? I know you're not a psychiatrist, or a chemist, but in a nutshell, for a layperson, what's actually happening in your brain when you take this stuff?"

"When people tell me their medications are working, they often say they feel like themselves, but a better version. When a negative thought starts, or something triggers their anxiety, the thought just peters out, instead of spiraling, because the medication is helping. So you have the thought, and instead of it ruining your day, it just dissipates. Medication, combined with cognitive behavioral therapy—the type of therapy that helps us question our thoughts and examine whether they're actually based in truth—is a real game changer for many people, in my experience."

I really liked Sarah's vibe. She had snake tattoos on her arms, knew about music and art, was a single mom, and was Jewish, like I am. She had kind, intelligent energy and clear green eyes. I felt safe in her hands. And when we talked, it flowed. She didn't seem to have an agenda, other than to get to the bottom of things.

"I've always wondered about the correlation between creativity and anxiety, Sarah. Like, when it comes to my mental illness, I wonder if it's like a chicken and egg situation? Do I thank my mental illness for how creative I am? Or do I have mental illness *because* I'm so creative? My engine, my fire, my desire to create—it all emanates from my desire to fill the emotional hole inside me. But what if there is no hole, Sarah? And if I fill it up, then what?"

"So you're worried that if you heal, it might make you less creative?"

Bingo.

"Yeah! Why do you think it's taken me so long to call you? You might ruin my business."

"I doubt that, Jeremy. I have a feeling just the opposite will happen."

I explained to Sarah that anxiety had walked side by side with me my whole life, so much so that I'd given it a name: Alan. Alan was always there, like that friend you once hung out with but who you've kind of outgrown. But I had to give Alan his props. He had, in a way, powered my success. Idea-makers like me are a dime a dozen; we have to jostle for competition, and I knew how much my rapid-fire thought processes had helped me get ahead.

"My anxiety is Nature's Adderall; it gets me pumped and focused, every day," I said. "I don't need drugs—I am drugs!"

"Salvador Dali said that."

"Yes, you're right."

I was thinking fast, talking fast, explaining how my anxiety had always propelled me to drive in the fast lane, helped me come up with my best ideas that had always emerged like Russian dolls, products of my racing mind, ideas that I would then paper-clip together, creating juxtapositions that were completely original, unheard of, new.

"Without my anxiety, I would never have started paper-clipping," I said.

"Paper-clipping? Like . . . stationery?"

"No! The paper clip mentality. It's the foundation of nearly every good idea I've had."

Paper-clipping is a way to shift the story, just by putting two unexpected elements side by side. Take two ideas from different worlds, and paper-clip them together. It's my Malcolm Gladwell shit, curated mania in the name of creation. Paper-clipping reminds us that innovation doesn't need to be made from scratch; it's all around us.

I stole this ideology for ideation from the ultimate thief, Andy Warhol, consummate paper-clipper. He took a can of Campbell's soup—a grocery product with zero artistic value—slapped it on a canvas, and created a piece of fine art that would one day sell for millions.

Soup + Canvas = Art.

When you work with a paper clip mentality, it opens up a world of creative possibilities. It creates sparks within the mundane. You just have to learn to move the goalposts, demolish the pillars of convention, and create your own rules.

Breakfast for dinner?

Why not.

Boozy cereal milk?

Yes.

Even humans are paper-clipped. We're a product of our parents coming together to create something new. I am my mom's French Caribbean Blackness and my dad's Middle Eastern Jewishness combined. I am her love of food and his passion for nightlife, paper-clipped together. Add to that the special sauce of my anxiety-fueled negative thought loops—and what you have is a recipe for success and disaster, all in one.

FRUIT LOOPS, LOOPY ANXIETY

Panic disorder, social anxiety, generalized anxiety, phobias, PTSD— there are many ways to tumble into an anxiety spiral, none of them fun. Worry ties your brain into knots, even as you're wondering, *what am I actually worrying about? What is actually happening in my brain that this vague concern was suddenly able to escalate into a full-blown panic attack and anxiety spiral?*

The anxiety story plays out across our bodies and minds, and ripples out into our social behavior, powered by reinforcing feedback loops wired in our minds that escalate the feelings, rather than diffuse them. Anything can trigger a spiral—stressful life events, general worries, or even a zit. The anxiety-prone mind will disproportionately focus on these thoughts, misinterpreting them as real danger rather than what they are—just stuff floating around your brain.

If the spiral boils over into a full-blown panic attack, certain physical sensations will be amplified. Your beating heart, butterflies in the stomach, and sweaty palms indicate you're about to lose control, causing even further panic.

A spiral converts abstract thoughts into *literal, physical* events in the body, via the hormonal system. Anxiety makes us respond to thoughts as though they are real, as though we are in imminent danger, which causes the brain to alert the body's glands to release adrenaline and cortisol, activating the sympathetic nervous system, resulting in a range of bodily sensations, all of which suck.

Being hyper-aware of these sensations, despite no actual danger being present, you begin to panic about the sensations themselves, entering a state of hyperarousal, experiencing increasing dread, triggering a fight-or-flight response even though there's nothing to fight, nothing to run from, except yourself.

More hormones are then released, accompanied by catastrophic thinking that tries to frame and explain intellectually why this particular moment, at a Grammy party or in a sushi restaurant parking lot, feels like the end of the world. These cycles build upon themselves in the long term, because the body and mind have now strengthened the false belief that certain thoughts, feelings, and sensations are to be feared. In the case of social anxiety or phobias, you might deliberately alter your social behavior in response to this spiral, and avoid the people, situations, or places that have triggered anxiety in the past.

Anxiety, viewed alone, is actually a pretty cool thing, something that's been fine-tuned by evolution over millions of years, and when it's working properly, it helps us survive in the face of danger. But for some of us, the ones with poor cognitive control, a tendency to internalize our feelings (yes, men, I'm talking to you), and those suffering from trauma and stress, our system becomes corrupted, like a hard drive, and that's what causes it to spiral out of control.

It starts in the amygdala located just above the temporal lobes of the brain. It governs how we perceive emotions, primarily fear, and it's all about survival. The amygdala maps emotional memories of learned reactions to past events so that we can recognize and respond to those events properly in the future. Something that happened to you when you were a toddler may be the reason you're feeling anxious today.

The amygdala will then initiate the fight-or-flight response, releasing stress hormones like adrenaline via the HPA (hypothalamic-pituitary-adrenal) axis, a nerve network that links the brain to the stress glands above your kidneys, flooding your entire body with anxiety. But there is an antidote: the prefrontal cortex of the brain, the part concerned with logical and rational thought, decision-making, and the formation of new memories. Activating this region of the brain will chill the anxiety and halt the spiral. But not all of us have a fully functioning prefrontal cortex, especially those of us who have experienced trauma.

When you have an anxiety disorder, it's as if your anxiety circuits are permanently switched on. Genetic predispositions to neuroticism (I know it's a stereotype, but did I mention I'm a Mizrahi Jew?), learned behavior, and past experiences all influence whether a person is at risk for developing anxiety. The good news is, there are very effective ways to treat and manage this fucked-up situation. Cognitive behavioral therapy helps people tackle the thoughts that trigger the anxiety spiral, allowing you to shut down anxious rumination before it triggers your body's entire hormonal system. Exercise, mindfulness meditation, and a diet that nurtures healthy gut bacteria all aid in emotional self-regulation. And then there are the meds. The SSRIs and benzodiazepines such as Valium that shut down the hormonal cascade that sets off the spiral.

All of the above was available to me.

And none of it appealed.

It wasn't a case of "if it ain't broke, don't fix it." It was a case of better the devil you know. And there was a big part of me that would have preferred to maintain the status quo. I was terrified of fucking with the engine of my creativity—my brain—in case I slowed it down.

FHALLING UPWARDS

My mom's name is Florence. She's mixed-race Afro-Caribbean—her family is from Martinique—born in Paris, and when she was around twenty, her best friend got a boyfriend whose best friend was a man by the name of Jean-Claude Fhal. My father.

Jean-Claude was a North African Jew who had emigrated to France in the 1960s from Tunisia with his parents, and when he met my mom in the late 1980s, he was a little bit of a ladies' man. Tan and chic with his Levi's 501s and blazer, he exuded style. His father was high up in the French military and his mother had worked in fashion, and from them Jean-Claude had inherited an alpha attitude and an impeccable sense of style.

He'd lived in Los Angeles for some years, selling denim. He went by "John Fall" instead of Jean-Claude Fhal, having learned early on that "exotic"-sounding names can sometimes work against you in the US. He met my mom while visiting family in Paris, and talked her into going back to the US with him, promising her a beautiful life in the shadow of the palm trees. She agreed, and I was born in August 1990, at Cedars Sinai hospital, the name on my birth certificate "Jeremy Fall," not Fhal.

By my third birthday, my parents' relationship was over, but the separation was amicable, and they continued living together, raising me in our apartment in West Hollywood, close to Fairfax Avenue, an enclave belonging to skaters and Hasidic Jews.

Both of my parents spoke French, and their native culture was different from the one I was growing up in. Most American kids have never seen their parents naked, for instance, but in my family, nudity was nothing to be ashamed of. American sons shake their fathers' hands, there's not a lot of hugging and kissing—but if you're French, kissing your dad on the cheek is completely normal.

Also, my father very openly kept a stack of *Playboy* magazines in his room, and it was no big deal. When I was six years old, he showed one to me. Pamela Anderson was on the cover, and inside, photos offered me my first introduction to the female anatomy. I liked what I saw, although I wasn't sure why. And I liked that my father was so open with me about grown-up things. There were no secrets in our household, and we could talk about anything over the kitchen table.

Quaaludes and cocaine—my dad made it clear those were things for grown-ups, and even though he liked them, I should stay away. Which I did, for most of my life. But I noticed that no matter how much my father consumed the things he liked—sex, fashion, drugs—nothing ever seemed to help him cross the line into satisfaction. He seemed happiest when he was reminiscing about the past, talking about the time when he roamed New York City as a young man, bartending at Mr. Chow's, hitting the dance floor at the Palladium, Limelight, and Studio 54.

At night, hearing the muted sounds of rails of blow disappearing up my father's nose behind the wall that supported my pillow, I knew I wanted the parts of him that were charming, decadent, witty, and stylish. His flaws were obvious, and I promised myself I would not inherit those. But my father and I shared a lot in common, I thought. We both wanted to be Somebody. To be on the list. To walk on red carpets, be rich, maybe build a Studio 54 of our own. Money, fame, success. I wanted to figure out how to get those things, somehow. For both of us. Then my mother told us we were moving to Acapulco, Mexico—and the dreams were put on hold.

My mother had found a job working for the luxury jewelry company Cartier, but as soon as we arrived in Acapulco, it turned out there was no job. I was hoping we would go straight back to LA, but she said no. She was going to look for another job in Mexico and try to make it work.

My dad had come with us but was living separately, and I hated that we weren't living together anymore. Dysfunctional as it might have seemed to outside eyes, I loved our broken family. So long as we were together, under the same roof, I felt safe. Now all that was gone, and here we were, in a new country where I couldn't speak the language, where my mom and dad were living apart for the first time in my nine years of life.

As a half-Black divorcée in a country where Black people and divorce were relatively unusual, my mom struggled to find work or friends. I also struggled to fit in. The new kid at school in Acapulco, I was the oversized, biracial Jewish boy with long hair in a room full of small-statured, short-haired Mexican Catholics. It was never going to work out. Unsure of myself, and my place in the world, I retreated further and further into my shell.

After three difficult months in Acapulco, we moved again. This time to a cartel neighborhood in Guadalajara. All our neighbors had AK-47s and they were friendly enough, for drug lords. But almost immediately after arriving there, I caught impetigo, a highly contagious bacterial infection that left my skin covered in yellow oozing sores. I felt dirty, diseased, and completely out of control. That's when my germophobia developed—to this day, I'm an obsessive hand-washer, paranoid about bacteria.

It wasn't all bad, though. And if there was one thing about my experience in Mexico that I remember fondly, it's the food. We didn't buy our groceries at Walmart; instead, my mom would buy us dinner from the street vendors, who sold freshly made *elotes* for a peso. They were delicious—corn, mayo, and cheese, who comes up with that? So simple, but so decadent! Years later, when I'd open restaurants of my own, I'd put *elotes* on the menu and have our cooks make them exactly the same way I remembered.

A few months into our new life in Guadalajara, a ten-year-old kid at my school pulled out a gun in class and shot the teacher in her head, killing her. I wasn't in the classroom, but the shockwaves spread throughout the school. I was terrified to go into class, and with that, my mom realized that maybe our time in Mexico had come to an end. When she said it was time to go home to LA, I'd never felt more relieved in my life, even though we were broke. It was just me and Mom, versus the world.

"We'll figure something out," she told me. And I knew we would. My mom was a survivor.

First, we lived in a motel in Hollywood. Then in a sublet on the Venice canals, which sounds chic now, but back then, Venice was fucking ratchet. Gang-infested and dangerous. We lived on two different couches, for a couple of weeks here, a couple of weeks there. Eventually, my mom found a one-bedroom in West Hollywood for me, her, and her new boyfriend, my soon-to-be stepfather, a French cook. (Not a chef, a cook, he took pains to tell me. In France, the word *chef* is only reserved for those who have spent a lifetime earning their stripes, running kitchens in fine establishments. Anyone using the word in vain might find themselves seriously looked down upon.)

I went back to school at the Lycée International, or LILA, a top-rated private international school in the leafy Los Feliz neighborhood. My French parentage meant I was automatically granted admission to a network of French private schools, and because my mother was a single parent, it meant I got a free ride. *La bourse*, the bursary, meant my exorbitant school fees were paid for by the taxpaying people of France. That's how my broke ass was able to receive a $15,000-a-year private education.

Vive la France.

My schoolmates were the children of diplomats and CEOs. They were from Belgium, Spain, Italy, and Portugal. They got BMWs for their sixteenth birthdays. Not me, though. I was on *la bourse*. Not that anyone knew, of course. That was my dirty little secret. Being the broke boy in a school full of rich kids, I had to get creative, just so I could afford the little treats my friends took for granted.

There was a soda machine on campus, for example. Back then, a can of Coke cost two quarters and a dime, and I didn't have two quarters and a dime, so I collected Pogs that came free in chip bags and sold them to my friends for a dollar. I did the same with Pokémon cards. My early business ventures on the playground meant I could drink as much soda as I wanted, and it felt good, making money of my own. Money helped calm the voices in my head that kept telling me I was nothing. Money gave me power and worth.

The kids at my school were big-time materialists who liked gossiping about everyone's financial status. *Bourse* kids were creatures to be pitied, somehow less human than students who paid regular tuition. I understood the nature of wealth-based elitism and decided the only solution was to lie. I told everyone I was the son of extremely wealthy parents whose work was too complex and top secret for me to discuss in any detail. For my entire education from the age of five to eighteen, rumors abounded that my dad was an arms dealer. Only a handful of my closest friends—all of whom were also on *la bourse*—knew the truth.

We were a tight-knit crew, the *Bourse* Kids. After school, we would hang out on Melrose, paint graffiti, shoot BB guns at cars, and burn ourselves by lighting fireworks. Stupid shit. Sometimes we would piss in one another's shoes, even though we grew up in sneaker culture, and sneakers were God. Imagine being a broke kid with a hard-on for $300 Air Jordans, when all you can afford are the five-for-twenty shoe deals at Footlocker. Imagine what that does to your already wounded sense of self-worth. I had swagger, but every time I looked at my feet, I knew the truth. I was pure *bourse* from the wrong side of the tracks. Nothing more.

My mom married her French cook boyfriend in 2002. He was running the kitchen at a café in Downtown LA called Angélique, and got my mom a job managing the place, which meant we could all move into a living space above the restaurant. I wished we could have set roots down somewhere else in LA, anywhere but Downtown, a barren wasteland. Angélique was on the corner of Eighth and Main, a block away from Skid Row, ground zero of addiction, poverty, and mental illness. I lived there from the age of ten until I was seventeen.

I knew the local prostitutes' names, and their hourly rates—forty dollars—because they would come in, grab a sandwich, and talk about their day. "Hi, sweetie," I'd say, and they'd laugh at me, this big kid in a man's body, barely twelve years old, as I bussed tables at the café. To this day, I say everyone should have a job in hospitality, at least once, because it teaches you *everything* you need to know about humans. And it gives you respect for those good souls who are capable of kindness because most of the time you are treated like absolute shit.

Sometimes I would see my parents' married friends circle the block, and I'd think, "Oh, he can't find parking." Then I'd see a woman getting in the car, and then I understood what was happening. Everything, everyone, could be bought and sold, I realized. And these were good people, good women, whom society had decided to toss in the trash heap.

A homeless guy named George—I'll never forget his name, and he's still on Skid Row as far as I know—often walked my mom and me home from the lot where we parked our car at night. If anyone tried messing with us, he would yell at them, "Get the fuck away!" Skid Row taught me a lot about life, about how easy it is to become consumed by your demons, and how the world doesn't care if you live or die when you don't have money. It made me so angry. Once again, the solution was clear.

So long as I make money, that'll never happen to me, or the ones I love.

At night, when the screams of lost souls and the wail of police sirens became too loud to bear, I'd go downstairs into the restaurant kitchen and comfort myself with a big, delicious sandwich. Sliced ham, cheese, tomatoes, cornichons, salami, lettuce, onions, olives, capers, mayo, and mustard—there were always enough ingredients on the sandwich prep table for me to get creative. Inventing my own recipes distracted me from the chaos outside, and with the chairs flipped on top of tables and the umbrellas stacked inside surrounded by locked metal gates, I felt calm and in control, king of my own little gastronomic empire.

My Sarahpist says it's common for anxious children to develop self-soothing mechanisms, and for me, food transformed the world from a frightening, unstable place into a universe of infinite and mouthwatering possibilities. Food made me forget we were still financially insecure and surrounded by illness and misery. Food helped me forget that every day I went to school, I had to make up new lies about who I really was, and where we really lived.

THE NIGHT A PAPER CLIP SAVED MY LIFE

One night, I didn't want a sandwich; I wanted French fries with something more interesting than plain old ketchup. I filled a bowl with Heinz ketchup and mixed in Worcestershire sauce, celery salt, Tabasco, and lemon juice. I dipped my finger in the reddish-brown goop and had a taste. *Damn, that's good.*

The perfect balance of spice, richness, and tang. Little did I know I was innovating my way to the prototype for my Bloody Mary Ketchup, which would one day become one of the most popular sauces in my restaurants. I called it Spicy Ketchup at the time because I was twelve years old and had no idea what the fuck a Bloody Mary was. I had a sense that my future lay in this. In creating experiences that tasted good. But how could anyone do that without being a cook, or a chef, like in France? I wasn't sure.

So I began playing around with other ingredients, making up recipes for more sauces. Some were inedible. Coffee ketchup? Disgusting. Vodka mustard? Way too intense. Marmite mayo? Even Brits wouldn't touch that shit. But what I was doing in the kitchen of my mom's café was more than just experimentation. Or a coping mechanism. I was building a conceptual blueprint for my future business. I was paper-clipping.

Condiment + Cocktail = Bloody Mary Ketchup

Father + Son = Holy Spirit

OR:

Random Element + Random Element = Two things paper-clipped to become a better thing.

In 2015, ten years after I came up with that ketchup, I had a come-to-Jesus moment. I was sitting in my car, eating McDonald's in The Grove parking lot. This is after Jared and I launched the King Eddy, and I knew I wanted out of nightlife, which had consumed me for the past ten years. I had begun to lose sense of who I was, and I was drinking heavily. I was depressed, and there were days I couldn't pull myself out of bed. I had become used to this cycle of upbeat, manic idea generation punctuated by slumps, and while I didn't mind the anxiety at the time, I really hated and feared the slumps. I wanted to erase them, and I knew getting out of the bar world was the first step.

"What do I represent?" I wondered, munching on my Big Mac. "Who is Jeremy Fall? What does he do? What does he like? How do I want the world to perceive me? What is my brand?"

I took another bite of my Big Mac, savoring the "special sauce." Just ketchup, mayo, and relish, paper-clipped. And that's when it hit me. *Food*. I was the Food Guy. I had *always* been the Food Guy, since I was a little kid, making that strange sauce in my mom's kitchen, paper-clipping. That's when I knew I wanted to do food, but within a context, a concept, an authentic vision that emanated directly from the core of my DNA.

What Studio 54 had brought to nightlife—innovation, high-low glamour, a cultural conversation—I wanted to bring to restaurants. I wanted to change the way people ate food, break the walls down, paper-clip ideas to design culture.

I had no experience in a commercial kitchen. I had never been to culinary school. Other than bussing tables at my mom's café, I had never worked in a restaurant. And I hated recipes. But it didn't matter. Food was my brand, my medium, because it was ME. I had to figure out how to express that part of myself through my business ventures, and write myself as a character into the story I wanted to read. So I made a paper clip, just like I had in my mother's kitchen. Spicy Ketchup had given me hope when I was a kid, and now Breakfast for Dinner would be the paper clip that saved me.

At the time, I was sleeping on an air mattress in a studio apartment with zero furniture. No AC, no heater. But Nighthawk was such a big hit, even though it was just eggs at night and booze in milk. The press were heralding me as some kind of boy genius, and when bloggers started calling me Chef Jeremy Fall, I got a little nervous, imagining my stepfather's reaction.

You're not a chef, you're just some kid who likes food, I thought.

But I went with it. Fake it till you make it. That's the Studio 54 formula.

I leaned into the smoke and mirrors, and let the paper clips lead the way.

A FLIGHT BACK TO OKAY

During the pandemic of 2020, I saw my industry completely crumble. Hot restaurants where it was once impossible to get a reservation went under and stayed empty for a year. I sold my restaurants. I couldn't hide behind work like I had for so long. The four walls that I thought were my reality became completely meaningless, and I found myself forced into a rare and unusual bubble of inactivity.

Meanwhile, I was beginning to really peel back the layers of myself with my Sarahpist. She was helping me unearth some realities that I'd been pushing away for years. Mainly that I was fucking depressed and super anxious, and had been for years, and the pandemic was amplifying those feelings until I couldn't bear it anymore. So on August 29, 2020, that's what I told the world. Via Instagram. I told them I was not okay, and needed a time-out while I figured out what to do with my head.

Signing off for a little while to focus on my mental health. As I navigate through a new chapter of my life, I like to think of change as a good thing. When it's reimagined as progress, our world, as it stands is going through a hard reset that's pulling us away from the meaningless things we used to worry about and teaching us about the importance of substance, silence over noise, selflessness over selfies, connections over distance, fresh air over red carpets, storytelling over posting stories. Self-reflection is one of the highest forms of wealth. And as we constantly inhale misinformation, distractions, and comparisons that make the future seem blurry, we need to remember that our growth lives in the exhale.

It was a few weeks after my thirtieth birthday.

What surprised me was how many responses I got. Mostly from men. Things like this:

"You put into words things I've thought about, too."

"You know, it's nice to see you talking about mental health. I've been embarrassed to talk about my own."

"I'm sorry you're going through this, I know we're not really allowed to be sad. Cause it shows a sign of 'weakness' and weakness is not 'masculine.' It's all bullshit. Thank you."

The pandemic was a time when a lot of people had to take a deep dive into themselves. We were left alone. Just us, and maybe our significant other, or immediate family. But a lot of people, let's say most of America, did not do the deep dive, and you could see the consequences unfolding on social media. People fighting, yelling at one another, ending years-long friendships. Many people suffered a terrifying loss of income, and were struggling to keep a roof over their heads. Who has time or money to devote to therapy and self-work when the planet is on lockdown and no one's sure what the future holds? Venting on social media seemed like the only thing left to do.

In general, whether we're in a pandemic or not, social media can be deeply triggering for anyone with an anxiety disorder. Comparing ourselves to other people feels even more painful if you're alone, especially when you're seeing baller types posting pictures from their yachts saying things like "OMG this is hard, but we're getting through it!"

Fuck. It's the kind of thing that'll make you wanna start a fight on Twitter.

Later that day, I called my Sarahpist.

"Sarah . . . I think I do need medication," I said, fighting back the feelings of shame and defeat.

"Jeremy," she said, "I'm very happy to look into that with you."

It felt odd, admitting my vulnerability out loud, in front of the world. And now, conceding defeat to being medicated, a fate I had dreaded for so long. But I had been doing this alone for so long. Pretending I was okay, when in reality I wasn't sure I'd ever felt "okay." None of it was working.

Healing, therapy, medication, meditation . . . fuck. Was this really me now? Was this the latest paper clip?

Jeremy + Treatment = ?

It felt scary, taking this step. But what was scarier was the thought of remaining stuck where I was.

One of the most dangerous aspects of any toxicity is that it's contagious, and leaders set the tone. We're all connected, and everyone's picking up on everyone else's unspoken feelings. If we're not admitting we're anxious but instead giving off an anxious, stressed-out, or domineering vibe, we're literally creating a chain reaction. We're polluting the psychic space with our disease, and not doing anyone any favors.

But how can you be honest in a way that doesn't make others shoulder the burden? What degree of emotion is appropriate to express? What's "healthy sharing" in a business environment? Because a lot of people, especially men in positions of power, don't share what's going on inside.

Mental health issues reveal themselves not just in relationships, but very much in the workplace too. People project their issues onto their peers, which can result in junior high dynamics in the boardroom, and family dynamics getting played out when you should be cooperating. If people don't do their own mental health work, it'll come out, and workplaces—God, especially kitchens—should be offering resources for mental health. On-site therapists, for instance, to meet with people and educate us on psychology. How we're often projecting our mom or our sister or our competitive dynamic with our brother onto the workplace. All these family dynamics tend to interfere with productivity, eventually, and the mental health of everyone else working there.

I've never started a meeting with "holy shit, everyone, I'm spiraling extra hard today!" But I have learned that it's appropriate to be transparent and honest about my anxiety and mental health, if only to empower the same transparency in everyone else I work with. Some of the most powerful moments of connection come about when we express our vulnerability and share our troubles. If I can admit "I'm anxious today" or "I didn't sleep well," it helps everyone else in the room understand that it's not their fault if I'm coming across as uptight.

When you think of boys in the schoolyard, we're subjected to certain kinds of play that test our ability to NOT express our feelings. Like, "I'm gonna make your mom a joke and you're going to get upset, but if you start crying, you're gonna be ostracized for it." So we're taught to be stoic, and our fathers typically don't offer much leadership in showing us how to be open, vulnerable males who are aware of their feelings. In fact, the vast majority of men have grown up with a real ingrained negativity towards sharing our feelings. It's something transgenerational and has been in our collective makeup for thousands and thousands of years. Vulnerability is something that we've been taught to despise.

My Sarahpist even has an equation, which I love.

"And by the way, Jeremy, intimacy consists of vulnerability and authenticity. People, whatever their gender, tend to be afraid of any kind of confrontation, any kind of vulnerability, any kind of intimacy. It just really isn't taught to us, in work, romantic, or sexual relationships. Vulnerability plus authenticity equals intimacy."

"Okay. I like it. I think it's correct and pretty hard to pull off. So vulnerability plus authenticity equals intimacy. And intimacy is, like, good."

"Yes, Jeremy, it's good."

"Remind me, Sarah—what are the benefits of intimacy for a human being?"

"Well, imagine being vulnerable, open, and authentic in your relationships. Once we are doing that, we're not holding on to stuff. We're not projecting as much. I understand that in workplaces, there are things that maybe shouldn't be discussed, or maybe you don't want these people knowing certain things about you. We definitely don't want to force intimacy on anyone. But if we can just start to shift toward a culture of, in general, valuing intimacy, and showing that this is an adult way of being, wouldn't that be good? Being an adult is being able to have hard conversations without people screaming or going off the rails. Understanding that you can be vulnerable and it doesn't mean you're any less of a man, or less of a leader. Knowing that you won't be attacked for your vulnerability, and trusting that you can have conversations without defensive reactions."

She was right. I want the people in my life to know that they can come to me and say I hurt their feelings, and for me to go, "shit, I am so sorry, let me look at my contribution to that." Rather than getting into, "well, here's why you're wrong," or "here's what I *actually* did." We all go into excuses, but excuses never feel good to the person who's hearing them.

My Sarahpist taught me that it's better to respond like this, when engaged in confrontation:

"I totally hear that. It's hard to hear and I might disagree, but what can we do differently next time? What do you need from me?"

We need leaders who are able to exhibit both warmth and strength as well as competence and credentials. And we need to remember that projecting strength before establishing trust runs the risk of eliciting fear, and creating a toxic environment. Nothing establishes trust more effectively than the emotional connection fostered through empathy and shared experience. This is why being open about your own anxiety or depression can be so powerful. It builds trust when you can ask the people around you "how are you?" without them feeling as if they have to lie or put on a happy face, because they know you understand.

This doesn't mean collapsing into a puddle of man tears during a Zoom call, or sending a group email about how your anxiety is deeply rooted in your parents' money troubles during your childhood. We can create models for living with anxiety, where it's possible to take care of our mental health, without anyone ever losing confidence in us.

My hope is that one day, in the not-too-distant future, I'll be living proof of that.

3

THE STUDIO 54 FORMULA

How to Be Authentically Inauthentic

AFTER DECIDING I WANTED MEDICATION FOR MY ANXIETY, I DID WHAT I ALWAYS did—I had anxiety about it.

"I'm scared I'm gonna lose myself, stop being creative," I said to my Sarahpist.

"That's a very common concern, but the right medication shouldn't affect your creativity," she said.

"I fucking hate psychiatrists. They're tools."

"Not all of them. I have a really great woman that I send all my clients to," she said.

"Maybe I should just go meditate in a forest."

HAVE I EVER meditated in a forest? No, I'm not going near a fucking forest, but my friend Yung Qualo has. He does it all the time. He's a musician, poet, and artist. He was one of the few guys I found myself able to talk with about mental health, at first. He told me the way he takes care of his mental well-being is to meditate and go on retreats. Breathing amid the stillness of nature, he finds peace, reconnection with his authentic self, and a sense of happiness. And obviously, as evidenced by the obscene number of mindfulness apps in the iTunes store, he's not alone.

Matthieu Ricard, a Tibetan Buddhist monk, has been called "the world's happiest man," and science proved it when neuroscientists from the University of Wisconsin monitored his brain waves with an electro-encephalography (EEG) test and found his mind had an "abnormally large capacity for happiness." Ricard responded by saying that anyone can achieve the same, just by freeing themselves of "afflictive emotions, such as hatred, craving, arrogance, jealousy, and mental confusion." Easier said than done, buddy.

As much as I'm not a meditating kind of guy, I've always envied those who can reach those peaceful states, unaided. For a long time, I couldn't even imagine being in a peaceful state. Anxious, depressed, moody, tormented, sure. The racing thoughts, the sense that I could never be enough, that the house of cards I had built around me was always on the verge of collapse—that was Jeremy, and I had just come to accept it. Even appreciate it. If I took away my angst, what would be left? A tall dude with no edge, no good ideas, and a raging appetite for cheeseburgers? Fuck.

I had always wanted to prove to the world that you really can be anything. That bullshitting is an art form to be mastered. I never realized, though, that you should make sure it's authentic bullshit, because that's exactly how my own mental health started to go awry. Literally, because I didn't keep my bullshit real.

I wore leather gloves to be fashionable, when I didn't really like leather gloves.

Social media allowed me to easily build an avatar of myself, and the avatar I chose to build was of a rich, trust-fundy kid who lived a glamorous life, like my friends from school, when in fact, the opposite was true. I'm not a trust-fund kid. But I had built a false self that looked very much like one, and now I was dealing with the repercussions, drowning in a sea of bullshit that I had created.

Still, meds? I just wasn't sure exactly how a pill was going to help me address several years' worth of lying to the world about who I really was.

"Look, Sarah, let's be real: the whole pharmaceutical industry is out to screw us over. Corporations are trying to take advantage of us, a hundred percent. We're overmedicating ourselves, trying to fix everything with pills because it's easy, it's quick. Meanwhile, Big Pharma is making a shitload of money. I mean look at that asshole, Martin Shkreli, inflating the price of insulin. You think he cares? You think—"

Mid-sentence, I sneezed, loud.

"Sorry about that," I sniffed.

I had a bad cold at the time and was doing everything I could to get rid of it. I was taking Tamiflu and shoving a neti pot spout up my nose several times a day, swirling salt water around my nasal cavities, while sucking on countless chemical lozenges and popping DayQuils for good measure.

My attempts to fight this cold had turned into quite the production, and as I sneezed again, that's when it hit me—here I was, pumping my body full of chemicals to rid myself of a cold that would last no more than seven to ten days, yet I still refused to treat the anxiety that had been fucking with me twenty-four hours of every day, seven days a week, for my entire life thus far, and possibly my entire future.

Hm.

Looking at it from that perspective, my reluctance to try anxiety medication did seem a little illogical. Perhaps my control issues were holding me back because I'd rather remain in the status quo of untreated mental illness than take a leap into the unknown of actual healing?

I knew medication wasn't going to cure the root causes of my anxiety, which lay in a plethora of shit—childhood trauma, brain chemistry, a lifetime of ignoring that I was sick. But medication could, perhaps, slow the spiraling thoughts. Maybe it would give me space to finally examine what was actually going on in my head, the real pain, the real bullshit. And then I could finally spend some time with the real me, no forest necessary.

CRAZY BEAUTIFUL FANTASY LIFE

It's hard to hold on to authenticity when you're climbing the career ladder. Like many ambitious creatives, I had always dreamed of being rich, powerful, successful, and recognized for my talents, and to get there, I'd spent my whole life pretending I already was those things, building an illusory self to manifest a new version of me. It's like what Anthony Bourdain talks about in his cameo in *The Big Short*, how when you have old fish that doesn't sell, just turn it into a stew, then it's not bad anymore, it's just different. That's what I did.

I schmoozed, I pretended, I winged it, I stretched the truth, I reimagined everything, and became a pro at creating ways to feel good about myself in completely inauthentic ways. I turned old fish into high-grade sushi, instead of just going with an honest stew, and eventually it made me sick.

I was a pathological liar up until my early twenties. About everything. Yes, *la bourse*, but I would even lie about the smallest shit, just to try to add value to myself. It could be anything.

"Have you seen this movie, Jeremy?"

"Yeah, of course."

I hadn't.

I went around school telling girls that I was a ninja in the kitchen, because my mom told me girls like men who cook. To my dismay, one of them called my bluff. I had invited her over to where we lived Downtown, thinking maybe we could hang out and listen to music, maybe make out. Turns out, she had only one thing on her mind. Food.

"You talk a big game, Jeremy Fall. Now, you're going to cook for me."

"Uh, sure!" I said. "You wait here, I'll get something started in the kitchen. How about a club sandwich?"

"A sandwich is not cooking. I want a real meal, Jeremy."

"My pleasure," I said, trying to sound smooth.

I went downstairs to the kitchen, ordinarily my safe haven, now a labyrinth of mysterious tools and implements I knew nothing about. I opened the fridge and pulled out some chicken thighs. No idea.

I called my mom, frantic.

"Mom, how the fuck do I cook chicken?"

She suggested a coq au vin and talked me through it step-by-step.

"Okay, Jeremy, turn on the stove."

"How do I do that? What does a pan look like? The black one or the silver one?"

There's a big difference between saying you cook and actually cooking, something that would come to haunt me, when, years later,

people started calling me chef or restaurateur, even though I hate recipes (because don't ever tell me what to do, I call the shots, I'm in control, and fuck yo recipe).

"Mom, I don't know what a cup looks like."

"It's in the third drawer, Jeremy."

In the end, I presented the girl with a plateful of burnt chicken,
which I attempted to redeem with a gigantic salad. It was horrible, but
she kissed me anyway. I knew I was a fraud and she did too, but it
didn't really bother me, yet.

You see, being inauthentic really fucking worked for me, at first.
Being inauthentic allowed me to take the empty space inside me and
project a complete fantasy upon it, and I did it with such confidence
and commitment that everyone bought in. Even me. Everyone believed
the illusion. I was just like Studio 54. An idea born out of nothing and
given form . . . through the power of sheer imagination.

RAGE AGAINST MY HYPE MACHINE

Studio 54 was one of the most iconic nightclubs in the history of
nightclubs, and I knew this because my father had told me all about
it throughout my childhood. He was there and had witnessed its mys-
tique firsthand. How, thanks to the famous clientele, inventive interior
design, and completely subjective door policy, Studio 54 had transformed an empty space (a three-story opera house and former CBS
studio on 254 West 54th Street, Manhattan) into an epic wonderland,
an iconic brand whose memory would survive long beyond its golden
era, from 1977 to 1980.

My father's eyes would always light up as he recalled the glamorous people in glamorous fashions—regulars included David Bowie,

Truman Capote, Divine, Salvador Dalí, Halston, Debbie Harry, Grace Jones, John Lennon, Andy Warhol, Lou Reed, and Richard Pryor—a who's who of twentieth-century art, music, and culture. It didn't matter how rich or famous you were, though, there was no guarantee you were getting in. You'd only get in if you were "cool." Before long, Studio 54's definition of cool was the only one that mattered.

The men who founded Studio 54, Steve Rubell and Ian Schrager, always made sure there were lines around the block, and kept people shivering outside in the winter cold for hours, even when the club was empty inside. Why? Rubell and Schrager weren't sadists, they were just really good at creating hype. Having lines outside made everyone want to be inside. That's human nature: we want what we can't have, and we yearn for acceptance and external validation because it makes us feel better about ourselves.

Listening to my father's talk about Studio 54, I thought, *if you can turn an empty space into a Studio 54, why not do that to yourself?* Why not manifest a version of yourself completely out of thin air, a version of yourself that is way cooler and more magical than the reality? Then all you have to do is get other people to believe in it. A little smoke and mirrors, a little fake it till you make it. Then I wouldn't be Jeremy Fall, the oversized, hairy, broke, pathological liar from a broken home—I could be Jeremy Fall, gatekeeper, tastemaker, Dionysus in black nail polish and overpriced sneakers. All it would take was a little creativity.

An important note on creativity: I didn't know I was actually "creative" until a few years ago. The word "creative" is very new to me. In fact, I was always told that I wasn't creative. I went to school with kids who drew and painted and were art kids. I was never that kid. Most of us are not blessed with artistic talent. But we all have the ability to imagine, if we dare. To dream. To pull something out of our asses and make it *the shit*.

When I was a kid, I wanted a pair of Adidas Kobe One sneakers. But I could only afford a pair of ratchet ass shoes from Payless Shoe Source. What I did was call them my Kobes, which then meant that I had Kobes, and no one questioned me. Reimagine everything, that's the core of all that I do, that's the core of branding, and the core of the Studio 54 formula. Lies, in fancy dress, for a good cause.

In order to Studio 54 myself, I would have to demolish the ceilings, rules, limits, and guidelines that society had set for me. Go to school, study, do well, kiss ass—nope, that wasn't going to be enough for a broke, mixed-race kid like me. The "right" way for me to build a life would be to remove all borders. Push every little hope about myself to the furthest and most impossible point, and then plant a flag in that. Innovate myself. Take the blank canvas and turn it into a masterpiece. Kobe's Mamba Mentality, plus the Studio 54 formula, is how "Jeremy Fall, Creative" was born.

BABY BOY'S FIRST GRAMMYS

If I was going to talk the talk, I'd have to walk the walk.

It was February 2006 and the Grammys were right around the corner, so with thoughts of Studio 54 in my mind, I decided to make my red carpet debut. I wasn't invited, obviously, but if I played my cards right, it wouldn't matter. Smoke and mirrors is what it takes, and I was ready to test out the formula, and get the social validation I knew I deserved.

I paid my friend Danny to show up to the Staples Center where the Grammys were taking place with his camera and told him to pretend to be a paparazzo. As soon as my taxi rolled up, he played the role to a T—freaking out when he saw me, just like we had planned, and acting like I was "somebody" while he snapped dozens of photos as I exited the car.

"Jeremy! Jeremy! Over here!" he yelled.

I stopped, posed for the camera, and acted indifferent.

Flash photography immediately creates an aura of glamour, and I knew that as soon as the other paparazzi noticed what was happening, they'd want to take my picture too.

"Who's that?" one of them murmured, while looking at this big kid in a tux in the crosshairs of his camera lens.

"No idea," I heard another paparazzo say.

It didn't matter. They started taking photos, and as they did, I gave them my very best celebrity face—furrowed brow, faraway look in my eyes.

When security saw what was happening, they, too, came under my spell and as if by magic, the barriers to the Grammy Awards melted away—these people were no match for my trickery, and not one of them suspected I was just some random teenager.

Paparazzi kept taking photos as I made my way along the red carpet, flashing lights indicating I was very close to reaching the pinnacle of everything I'd ever dreamed of. It's a beautiful thing, being so young and feeling like you're somebody. I found myself filled with a natural glow, and I was sure that anything I touched would turn to gold. The fear, the excitement, the anxiety, the strength, the thirst to battle anything and everything in my way and make it all come true; this was a high like no other. I enjoyed every single millisecond of it and thought, *this is what success feels like. This is what really matters.*

I strolled inside and nodded my head to say hello to other Grammy guests. I introduced myself to record label heads, music producers, and movie stars—people I still know and work with today. VIPs milled around like it was a family BBQ, and I felt strangely at peace. This was home.

Moments before the ceremony started, I walked right up to an usher and, making sure no one I knew heard me, I said, "Hello. I'm a seat-filler. Where should I go?"

Every major awards ceremony in Hollywood hires seat-fillers, meaning people who sit in empty seats so the auditorium always looks full on camera. Like I said, smoke and mirrors, name of the game. The usher guided me to a seat next to a well-dressed—and well-known—industry couple. I said hello to them and settled in to watch the show. For a split second, I completely forgot I wasn't supposed to be there, and that, my friends, was the gateway drug. The best fucking feeling in the world. "I'm not afraid of anything anymore," I thought. "I've found what I love and I'm never going to give this up."

After the awards ceremony, I made an attempt to get into the Governor's Ball, a seated dinner, and the guy managing the list politely told me to fuck off. I was high on confidence, though, and I didn't care. My work was already done, anyway. I made it to the Grammys, sat in the audience, and drank the damn champagne. In Hollywood, that's all that matters. It's something you can literally build a career on, a fake ass rinse and repeat until you, and everyone else, forgets where the "fake you" ends and the "real you" begins.

I stood on the corner of the street, waiting for my "paparazzo" buddy to pick me up and take me home. With a crumpled suit jacket flung over my shoulder and a clutch of business cards in my back pocket, I wondered how I could continue living up to this person I had created for the Grammys that evening.

"I'm going to need a Rolex, like Paul Newman's in the film *Winning*," I thought. "Then I'll need a Porsche, because Porsches are fast and cool, and Dad always loved those."

Most of all, what I needed and wanted more than anything in the world was to make *Forbes* magazine's "30 Under 30" list. Seeing my name on that list would be conclusive proof that I, Jeremy Fall, was Somebody. The "30 Under 30" was a surefire defense against the destiny I had been trying to avoid all my life.

Just like an addict in the blissful early throes of their disease, I began to fixate on ways that I could feel the very same high once again. I was addicted to the status that comes with external validation, even when that status has little to do with reality. So, like all addicts, I had to come up with a way to get my fix again.

It wouldn't take long.

About a month after I crashed the Grammys, I came up with a genius idea.

"I want to start a summer nightclub for kids," I announced to Danny, my personal paparazzo and fellow *bourse* kid.

"A nightclub?"

"Yeah."

If you're aged between twelve to seventeen years old, summers in Los Angeles can be long and very boring. There's nothing to do at night, other than go to the movies. A nightclub for bored ass teens was exactly what this city needed.

"Have you even been to a nightclub, Jeremy?"

"No, but I know how they work. Believe me."

"So how are you going to do this?"

"My dad says most clubs are closed on Monday nights. I bet I can find one that'll let me do an all-ages night on Mondays. Every high school kid in LA would come. I mean, it's not like there's anything else for them to do."

"Yeah!"

Danny's brother had a friend named Josh who happened to be an event promoter, and Josh knew who I was, because he lived in Downtown LA and was a regular at Angélique, my mom's café.

I was bussing tables one afternoon when he waved me over.

"So I hear you're starting an all-ages club night?"

"Uh, yeah. Totally."

"Did you find a venue yet?"

"I'd love to do something at the Avalon, have you heard of it?"

He laughed.

"Of course I've heard of the fucking Avalon, Jeremy."

The Avalon was one of the hottest clubs in Hollywood, at the intersection of Hollywood and Vine, across the street from the Capitol Records building. It's where all my rich school friends with money and fake IDs would go. In the 1980s, it was called The Palace, a mega dance club known for having the most expensive light and sound system in town. Prince, Madonna, and the Rolling Stones regularly partied at The Palace, and people called it the West Coast version of Studio 54.

"The Avalon could be interesting," Josh said, handing me his card. "My friend Ryan and I are promoters and if we partner up, I'd like to invest in your idea. We can negotiate with the club on your behalf. Oh, and we're working with DJ Shadow on some projects. I could see how much he'd charge to DJ your night."

What. I fucking loved DJ Shadow.

"Sure. Great. I'll get back to you."

That afternoon, I started my first LLC, Mad City Entertainment. Then I called Josh and agreed to partner with him and Ryan on a new, all-ages club night for bored LA high-schoolers, with DJ Shadow behind the decks. I would call the night Verge. Red Bull provided nonalcoholic cocktails, and I sold tickets to kids from different high schools across LA at twenty dollars a pop.

Josh and Ryan invested $20,000 into the night, and I agreed to a $1,250 flat fee, which was insane money to me. There were no contracts because I was a kid and didn't know what the hell I was doing. Just a verbal handshake and a giddying sense that, finally, I was about to do something that would help me live up to the bullshit I'd been telling the world about myself all these years.

I worked solidly for three months, from April through July, promoting my glorified school dance on Myspace. I was adding, adding, adding friends on that platform. I wound up with 10,000 friends, which, back then, meant you were the tits. The coolest motherfucker. It felt like fame, even though I wasn't actually anyone. But everyone was doing it. All the early Myspace stars. Jeffree Star, Audrey Kitching. Dirk Mai, who was Audrey's photographer and became one of my best friends. Clint Catalyst. Cory Kennedy and her boyfriend, photographer Mark the Cobra Snake, Shepard Fairey's intern. A whole gaggle of us in LA, unknowingly following in the footsteps of my hero Andy Warhol and Studio 54, concocting our own fifteen minutes of fame out of thin air thanks to this new thing called social media.

On Myspace, I could see how other DJs and promoters were becoming stars, and how electroclash music had gotten where it was. I became obsessed with the French artists like Justice and Daft Punk, and I shared the music with my friends.

On July 23, I borrowed my mom's car and drove to the Avalon, wearing a white Abercrombie button-up shirt, brown corduroy True Religion jeans, and boots. I walked into the venue early, excited. It was so big! A guy called Preston introduced himself to me as the director of promotions and events.

"Hi, Jeremy, we're excited to work with you on this. If it goes well, maybe we can do more."

"Oh yeah! I'm telling you, there's a new wave of music, it's going to be huge, called electroclash, have you heard of it?"

"Yeah, of course."

"Well, there's these guys from Paris, their name is Justice, there's this other guy named Steve Aoki who you totally book, and all the Ed Banger guys, those are like my fucking people. Benny Benassi, you know?"

"Actually, not familiar with him."

"You will be."

I was talking to him like I had been doing this all my life. I was so used to bullshitting and hyping myself, it was like I was born for nightlife. It felt like I could do no wrong—until the doors opened, and it became clear that Verge was a bust.

Yes, I had sold 220 tickets generating $4,400 in ticket sales, but I'd had eyes bigger than my stomach. This was a 1,500-capacity venue, and it felt empty inside. I was so bummed. It was my first reality check. Ryan wasn't happy. He lost a shitload of money that night, and I didn't get paid my full rate. Studio 54 this was not.

"Don't worry, Jeremy, Rome wasn't built in a day," my dad said.

Then, a few months later, I got a phone call from an unknown number on my black and white T-Mobile Sidekick.

"Is this Jeremy Fall?"

"Yes?"

"Hey, this is Preston, director of promotions at the Avalon. I know that thing didn't work out, but we really liked your ideas. We'd love to do something with you."

And that's how I became an intern at the Avalon. Within weeks, I was counting cash until 4 a.m., booking artists like A-Trak, Drop the Lie, Hyphy Crunk, and Justice. I started building a name for myself and a reputation for booking fun, packed nights. I could text Gaspar from Justice and invite him to do a last-minute surprise DJ set, which was a regular thing back then, and DJs were doing it for free. I even booked Lady Gaga for $300 in 2006 at the Avalon, for our night Tiger Heat. We had a night called Avaland—Saturday was 18+ and Sunday was 21+, back-to-back identical all-nighters where we'd stop serving at 2 a.m. then start again at 6 a.m.

I'll never forget the party I threw for DJ AM (rest in peace). Will.i.am was DJing, and at the end of the night Lindsay Lohan was cutting loose, as always, dancing on a stripper pole at Spider Club upstairs until five in the morning. The place had closed and she stayed longer with her friends, and they were taking turns dancing on the stripper pole until six in the morning. I wound up taking my VIPs to an after-hours at the Dime on Fairfax, where Jessica Simpson and Lindsay Lohan got into a fight, because their stylists had gotten into a fight. Everyone was throwing stuff at each other, and I thought, *this is exactly where I want to be.*

I was still living with my mom, and God bless her, she supported me all the way. "As long as your grades are up, Jeremy. I'm not going to stop you from being you." Finally, I knew who I was. I was Jeremy Fall, nightlife impresario, and my timing couldn't have been better.

See, in the mid- to late-2000s, Hollywood club land was in the midst of a renaissance, driven by celebrity. On any given night, Britney

Spears, Ashton Kutcher, Jessica and Ashlee Simpson, Paris Hilton, and Lauren Conrad and her costars from MTV's hit reality show *The Hills* would frequent a trifecta of Hollywood nightlife venues—Hyde, Area, and Les Deux.

Thanks to my success with the Avalon, I found myself running the door at all three clubs, depending on the night. Yes, I was still sixteen years old. I guess the owners must have just forgotten to ask me my age; but why would they? I was six foot seven inches tall with facial hair to match. I looked about thirty-five. I carried myself with so much confidence that no one would suspect I was still in high school. The Studio 54 formula was really working, and I used it to wrangle my way into managing the hottest velvet ropes in Hollywood, operating with a calm, adult decisiveness completely beyond my years.

"Hey, Jeremy, I need a table for eight tonight."

It was Lauren. Or Ashton. Or Lindsay.

I'd respond straightaway, "Sure, I got you."

I had notes in my phone next to every VIP's name. I knew their favorite table. I knew if they preferred gin, vodka, or rum. I knew their birthdays, always making sure they had candles and cake. The Les Deux guest list was a who's who of 2000s tabloid pop culture: Heath Ledger and Michelle Williams, the Olsen twins, Hilary Duff, Mischa Barton, Tara Reid, Johnny Depp, Orlando Bloom, and Jay-Z (who would also get up and rap). Lady Gaga once arrived in a tiny bikini bottom and high heels. One minute, Beyoncé was dancing in the aisles, and the next, Prince would be hanging out sipping on water. Kim Kardashian held her twenty-seventh birthday party at Les Deux with her entire family there. Britney Spears frequented Les Deux so often that she asked if she could fill out an application for work.

The stars of Young Hollywood partied in the club's outdoor area, which was basically a converted parking lot. Afterwards, they could be spotted stumbling from the club's doors through the lenses of flashing cameras as their Escalades waited outside. It was inside, though, where they were safe from harassment. Inside, they could be their rich, beautiful, perfect selves. And I was the gatekeeper to this super cool Shangri-La, where the famous would mingle with the infamous, and where those who were simply rich bought their way in, dropping thousands of dollars a night on bottle service like it was no big deal.

Celebrities would often get free tables, but everyone else would drop serious cash to party. At the clubs where I worked, a bottle started at a thousand dollars; three thousand for Dom Pérignon. The nightly average for a table was ten to fifteen thousand dollars, and sometimes it would even reach two hundred thousand dollars.

Looking back, I think part of the reason people liked me is because I didn't run the door simply based on whether you were famous or whether you had money for bottle service. You'd also get in if you were cool, or if you had the right vibe—just like the stories I'd heard about Studio 54 from my father. That was the energy I wanted. Being rich, beautiful, and famous helped, but so did your coolness and creativity. I didn't care what someone did for a living, or how much money they had—if they gave a shit that night about how they were dressed, and came out with a good attitude, they were probably getting in.

It got to the point where the only way to get into the clubs was to know me. And everyone who was anyone did know me. Or at least, they got to know the person I was showing them—door Jeremy, Les Deux Jeremy, arbiter-of-cool Jeremy. But did they really know anything about me? Did they know I had a history test the next day, or that I went home to a modest apartment above my mom's café next to Skid Row? What people knew was the fantasy version of Jeremy Fall. The alter ego. The bullshit upon bullshit. Mountains of it. I went big, because that was how desperate I was to find some sense of self-worth.

Every Thursday night, the main cast of *The Hills*—Lauren Conrad, Heidi Montag, Spencer Pratt, Whitney Port, Brody Jenner, and Kristin Cavallari—were at the club. There came a point when my sixteen-year-old mind realized that Jeremy Fall's entire currency was based on the fact that I knew these people and they knew me, yet an invisible line existed between us. I was doing my job, and they were being rich, perfect, and famous. I understood the difference, and for a long time, it didn't bother me. Just being around celebrity culture was enough to feel like I had made it and I had value.

Then I watched the show and started to wonder if, just like everyone else in America, I was this person on the outside looking in. That's when I heard that voice in my head for the first time. A voice belonging to an invisible, malevolent entity taking up headspace. I called him Bob, and I'll never forget his first cruel words to me: "You may get to choose who passes the velvet rope, but you'll never belong on the other side."

Self-loathing welled up in me, and my thoughts began to race. Even though I was exactly where I wanted to be, for some reason it wasn't making me feel good. In a way, it was making me feel worse. And this is the problem with the Studio 54 formula. It really does work, but it doesn't always lead a person toward happiness, or authenticity. And the further we drift from our true selves, the higher the likelihood that a sense of unease will begin to permeate our every waking hour.

The more successful I became, the more removed I was from my sense of self. Rich, powerful, successful, and badass—I spent my whole life pretending to be those things, and only once I had them all did I realize they don't really matter when you're out of your mind.

WHO INVITED BOB TO DINNER?

Have you ever noticed a nagging inner voice? The one that tells you what you should (or should not) be doing? Maybe this voice says shit like "who do you think you are?" or "what makes you so special?"

Sometimes, the narrative can actually be motivational and propel you toward some goal. Problem is, when you reach it, you might believe your effort or achievement is not enough. The goalposts keep moving. And you have Bob—or whatever you call your inner critic—to thank.

There's an upside and a downside to Bob. Bob has an appreciation for high quality and meeting goals. Bob loves learning and accomplishments. But Bob's big problem is that he has no internal sense of core self-worth. Everything Bob cares about is tied to meeting others' expectations. He's unrelenting in his obsession with external validation, on social media and from peers, and his standards are based on an unrealistic and stringent pursuit of worthiness.

Failure is forbidden because Bob is obsessed with earning approval and acceptance based on wealth, people-pleasing, looks, and accolades. Bob tells me I am only worth what I accomplish, and how well I accomplish it. Nothing else matters, except what people think.

Bob brings with him fear and anxiety, rooted in the belief that I am never doing enough, and never deserving of what I already have. Bob exists within the same negative mind loop as Alan, my anxiety. Together, they form a chorus of naysayers and judges, constantly pointing out my weaknesses and flaws, always telling me to quit, before I get found out for what I am.

A fucking fraud. Smoke and mirrors.

And it was easy for me to believe him, because in some way, I knew he was right. I had built my identity on a series of lies and exaggerations, and one day, they would collapse.

THE ART OF BEING AUTHENTICALLY INAUTHENTIC

Authenticity is a big thing for my Sarahpist. It comes up a lot. And of course, when I started telling her about Bob, and the things he'd said to me over the years, she had a LOT to say.

"If you hinge your entire sense of self-worth on external validation, and create a false self in order to get that validation—oh boy," she said. "You're setting yourself up for a lot of anxiety and depression. Even if you don't truly believe in yourself, the key is to try to fill your cup halfway, and that halfway has to be that you find concrete reasons to like yourself, no matter what anyone else thinks. Self-love is a life's work, right? And beyond saying nice things to yourself in the mirror every morning, it helps to do 'esteemable acts.' Things that make you feel good about yourself, like volunteering or just doing things where there's nothing in it for you other than, you know, feeling good. Caring for others is one of the best ways we begin to care for ourselves. We have to be able to do these 'outside-in' things, these esteemable acts for ourselves in the world. And we have to do the 'inside-out' work, which is working in therapy, or with a coach, or reading self-help books, or meditating—whatever you need to work through your issues, so you're okay with who you authentically are. If we don't do that, then we're operating with an empty cup, and we're going to rely on the entire external world to fill our cup the whole way—and that's a dangerous, highly insecure place to exist in."

"Okay, I get it—so I should just be independent, and not care what other people think about me?"

"No, that's not what I'm saying. Humans are interdependent beings. And there is such a thing as toxic independence, which often goes hand in hand with a hyper-masculine take on mental health, where you should be hyper-independent, not care what anyone thinks. But aren't we the product of the survival of thousands of years of inter-dependence? It can be toxic to be hyper-independent, which is why I say we have to build a cup halfway. If you go too far in the direction of completely relying on other people, then you swing into an empty cup and hyper-dependence, but if your cup is full of yourself, there's not going to be much for anything—or anyone else."

"Huh. Seems like toxic independence feeds into some of the issues with American individualism, basically? This idea of being a strong, silent, lone ranger kind of person who doesn't give a fuck. Society holds that up in a way, tells us it's good to not give a fuck what anyone else thinks of you. But that's not to say that you shouldn't give a fuck about anyone else."

"I do think the line gets blurred, Jeremy."

So basically, she was saying that what other people think of me is not my problem, but that doesn't mean I should go out in the world and be an asshole. I can't control what other people think of me, but I can show up in a way that is ethical and kind and human—and I can show up for myself, and make sure my cup is filled to the halfway mark, at least.

I've often heard that you can't love anyone until you love yourself. Because I'd been operating on an empty cup for so long, filling up with externals, I wondered if this meant I'd never actually loved anyone. The thought made me feel profoundly sad. Here's what my Sarahpist had to say.

"Sure, there's a grain of truth in that you can't fully care for another person if you really fucking hate yourself. But I think it's bullshit to say that you have to fully love yourself in order to experience love. You would never say that to a baby—oh, you're not worthy of love until you love yourself. And it plays into that idea of hyper-independence, which contributes to avoidant behaviors, especially in men. All this does is rob people of the opportunity to enjoy intimacy and support."

I was beginning to wonder about this house of cards that we've built for ourselves. One in which we're so terrified of vulnerability and inter-dependence that we normalize the fact that anxiety, depression, and suicide are on the rise, especially among men. When the shit hits the fan, if there's no culture in our lives that shows us it's okay to ask for help filling or emptying our cup a little, the same patterns are going to keep repeating through each and every generation. Chronic unavailability. Fear of being intimate. Not being able to trust that we can metabo-lize pain, openly. Not having the tools to deal with failed marriages or breakups, because we're not sure how to seek resources. Not being able to just have a talk when something's bothering you, knowing that it's not going to escalate into physical or emotional violence. Trusting that it's okay to share your feelings and no one's gonna freak out on you or get defensive. I'd always grown up with the cliché that men hate to talk, but it's just not true. All you need is a few positive experiences to realize that wow—talking about our feelings actually makes things better.

I've found, over the years, it's impossible to be all authentic, all the time. But if you can just figure out how not to lie to yourself, that's a huge start. You can separate your fake career self, Jeremy Fall LLC, from Jeremy Fall, the person. Your job shouldn't define who you are, it's what you do. And if sometimes you have to be an actor, that's okay. You can pretend to be successful, confident; you can create yourself to be whoever you want to be, just don't blend the worlds. When I was sixteen, I was running as fast as I could from my real self. Trying to convince Jeremy that he was Jeremy Fall LLC, trying to make them be one person. And that's where I started to struggle, because no one can lie to themselves forever without going crazy.

Of course, the feelings were far too confusing to process at age sixteen, working the door at Les Deux, so I buried them and got back to work, smiling at the creatures of the night, continuing the massive rebranding project that was Me. Marketing, reimagining, spinning, paper-clipping, filling empty spaces with all my dreams.

It wasn't until I learned to observe the inner dialogue, with the help of my Sarahpist, that I began to recognize Bob for who he was. A sadist. When I wrote down the words he'd fill my head with, I was shocked at how rude and cruel he really was.

"You're not supposed to be here, Jeremy. Who do you think you are?"

Bob was tightly wound, compulsively critical, a nagging buzzkill hellbent on reminding me that I was a failure who should be ashamed of who he is.

Only through therapy did I begin to realize the difference between Bob and myself. And before long, I began to turn down his volume.

"You came from nowhere, are you sure you belong in this room with all these fabulous people?" he'd ask.

"Yes, Bob. I've got this," I'd reply, adding, "Why don't you break for lunch?"

4

FUCK YOUR RECIPE

Bespoke Methodologies for Not Giving a Fuck

D ON'T GIVE ME RECIPES. DON'T EVER TELL ME WHAT TO DO. I CALL THE SHOTS. I am in control. Fuck your recipe.

I know I sound triggered, so forgive me, but that's because after years of trying to follow other people's recipes, I had to learn the hard way to honor my own palate and tune in to who I really was as an individual. Easier said than done, when you're a young broke kid in Hollywood who thinks the only way to get ahead is to NOT be himself and follow everyone else's recipe for what it means to be successful.

What I learned in the kitchen taught me a lot about life. To tweak recipes so they fit me, and not the other way around. To stop believing someone else's idea of what tastes good is more valuable than your own. The longer you do that, the less chance you'll ever know the satisfaction of creating something that is truly, authentically yours.

This is how I cook a steak. Maybe it's not how you cook a steak, but this is how I do it, and it is truly, authentically mine. Check it out.

First, I make sure it's at room temp, then I season the shit out of the meat on both sides. I put a cast-iron pan in the oven and heat it up to five hundred degrees. I take it out, put the pan on the stovetop, and turn the flame up to the max. I drop the steak in the pan. No butter, no oil, no nothing. I sear it. I throw in a shitload of butter, garlic, and rosemary and let it cook. Then I throw it back in the oven to finish it. I let it rest for ten minutes, under foil. Then I drizzle olive oil and sea salt over it, and it's the shit. This is how I do it. It works for me because it's my recipe. It's tailored to my specific likes and dislikes regarding how a steak should taste.

Let's think about making a sandwich. My perfect sandwich is never going to be identical to anyone else's perfect sandwich. The thickness of the bread. The kind of cheese. Is it toasted? What kind of toppings and sauces are you using? There are a million types of pickles. There is no one way to make a sandwich, as Subway figured out a long time ago. There's only YOUR way, and when you slavishly follow someone else's vision, it'll never taste quite right. You'll never be able to live by that sandwich, and that sandwich will always leave you feeling unsatisfied.

AMERICAN IDOLS

During the first half of my career, I was so obsessed with not being Jersey Fall, I zeroed in on icons. Celebrities. People who had the things I didn't.

Fame.

Success.

Coolness.

Cultural currency.

But as I learned, emulation can lead you down some dangerous paths.

All innovators stand on the shoulders of others, and it's okay to follow in the footsteps of those who have done great things before you. It's okay to be inspired by your predecessors—all you have to do is remember, you'll never actually *be* them. And if you copy them entirely, you'll just be a replicant. A photocopy. An echo. Your work will feel derivative, and when you're someone who aspires to creativity and originality, that's the worst possible insult.

Even Andy Warhol, who based his entire career on reproductions of existing ideas, did so in a way that was truly original. That is the job of the creative—to tap into the core of your own unique DNA, maybe paper-clip it with something, add some Studio 54 hype, and present the world with ideas that feel fresh, unique, and undeniably YOU.

Inauthenticity led me into unhealthy psychological territory, and for a while, I worried I was trapped there. That my business and creative identity would remain forever caged within the boundaries of a persona I developed when I was mimicking other people. In my case, the rich kids at the Lycée, the celebrities on the Hollywood scene, and a panoply of other American idols.

I modeled my goals and aspirations around the spirit of Les Deux and *The Hills*, pretending I was as rich and glamorous as they were, so I could one day be the same as them. Those were my role models because they represented fame, status, and money, even though those brands were based on hype, on thin air, on PR spin. I'm still amazed that I thought these would be healthy role models for someone like me.

Andy Warhol is perhaps the artist who has influenced me the most, but he was also a compulsive liar. Maybe it was because of the difficulties he suffered as a child—growing up in poverty as the son of immigrants, or developing St. Vitus's dance, a neurological disorder characterized by writhing and explosive involuntary movements, at age seven. His survival mechanism was to live in a fantasy that he turned into reality, to celebrate lies, branding, and the illusions perpetuated by fame.

He became brilliant at creating iconic art from nothing, as he did from a Campbell's soup can, but the difference between Andy Warhol and the rest of us, perhaps, is that he was actually comfortable inhabiting a space of falseness. He felt at ease there because he was always honest about it, and always honest about the fact that much of the American Dream is built on spin, where the shaping of narratives to support an idea may or may not be rooted in reality.

Warhol once said, "If you want to know who I am, just look at the photos. That's me, there's nothing else."

He was inspired by the facades that we create for ourselves in order to be seen and feel like we matter in the world. Inauthenticity was his preferred subject matter, and he owned it in a truly authentic way. That was his recipe for success. But inauthenticity wasn't working for me. It was turning me into an anxious, angry, self-loathing man. I did my best to be Andy and follow his lead. But unlike Andy, I didn't have the tools to take control of that narrative, and ensure it didn't wind up leading me in its own direction, not mine.

YES, CHEF

I'll let you in on a secret.

I never really understood why Nighthawk was such a big hit. I mean, it was eggs at night. Booze in cereal milk. I had never gone to culinary school. I'd never trained in a kitchen. I was just some guy with a lot of cool, simple ideas that worked. The more people complimented me on my ingenuity, the more I wondered if they were just being polite. Behind my back, were they saying I was overrated?

Then one day, I got a call saying I'd been invited to cook my favorite Nighthawk recipes on Guy Fieri's Food Network show, *Diners, Drive-Ins and Dives.* One of the highest-rated cooking shows on American TV.

Fuck.

Don't get me wrong. I loved that my business idea had blown up this much, but I never imagined myself cooking on national TV. All I could think about was that chicken I cooked for my teenage crush, the feeling of guilt when I realized she knew I had been lying about my culinary skills. I hadn't enjoyed the feeling then, and I knew I'd enjoy it even less when it was being broadcast to a billion homes around the world.

"I'm worried—I'm not a cook, I've never even worked in a kitchen," I told my publicist.

"You'll be fine," she said.

"I mean, I definitely know how to boil water."

"You're going to be great, Chef Fall."

Chef Fall? Who the fuck was this person? Should I just go with it?

I did know my way around a kitchen, somewhat. I'd worked on developing all those Nighthawk dishes with my business partner at the time. But I was no "chef." I had not undergone years of training. There's no such thing as a twenty-three-year-old "chef" in Paris. But in America, the rules are different. The terms are looser. You do one cooking show, you open one restaurant, you're a chef.

God bless America, and fuck my life.

The day before the shoot started, I spent eighteen hours in the Nighthawk kitchen learning every single one of those recipes from my staff. I wanted to learn how to hold the pots and pans so I looked like a pro. How to cut things. How to stir. How to make sausage and biscuits look effortlessly cool.

The Food Network wanted to see me make everything from scratch, which meant I had to learn how to cook and break everything down into twelve different steps. I made biscuits, pork belly, and French toast—the toast was a bit easier, but it was coated in Rice Krispies.

It would take two days of shooting to film a seven-minute segment, and when those cameras turned on, it was like an out-of-body experience.

I, Jeremy Fall, am the best chef in the whole damn world, I told myself, forcing myself to believe my own hype, unleashing the Studio 54 formula on this situation. And it worked. Even though I was literally acting, I came across as real and authentic, and I made those dishes like I'd grown up in a kitchen. It was at this point that I think I realized just how thick the shield of bullshit around me was. How could anyone see who the real me was, behind that, even me?

My career had always been my "fuck you" to a world that looked down on people of color, people who grew up broke on *la bourse*, people who were Jewish, people who were male and wore black nail polish and liked to wash their hands a lot. For years, I'd been chasing career goals in order to feel validated. Boxes on a checklist were my currency for happiness, and in escaping my fear of being a Nobody I had damned myself to a life spent climbing up an infinite ladder towards . . . more bullshit. I would never be Andy Warhol, but here I was, Chef Jeremy Fall, nothing more than a sales and branding exercise built on smoke and mirrors. I had become my own Studio 54, except on the Food Network, and I wasn't sure how I felt about it.

The more successful I became, the more the doubts and anxiety crept in. A sense of fraudulence continually overshadowed my ability to enjoy my successes, to believe the numerous validations of my so-called abilities. No matter how high I rose up the ladder, it seemed like I couldn't quite internalize my accomplishments, something I would later learn is extremely common among high-achieving, successful people.

I was completely incapable of truly enjoying my success. I downplayed my wins and had a hard time accepting compliments. Worst of all was this sense that I'd have to live with this forever. This fear of being "found out," of being unmasked, haunted me.

Yes, I had worked hard for years to get where I was. Yes, everything I had earned was real and legitimate. But still, there was this disconnect and I felt myself floating in this strange and fascinating space, one in which I was constantly asking myself, *how long do I have to keep pretending to be a Food Guy when there are real chefs out there, working their asses off? Are they judging me?*

By that point, of course, it was too late. I'd created a version of myself that was very real and was earning me money, not to mention the fame and accolades that I'd wanted all my life. And slowly I found myself hating it, and hating myself. I was trapped inside Jeremy Fall, and I couldn't see a single damn way to get out.

Around then, I started to realize that in the creative fields, there is no set pathway other than the one you carve out for yourself. You can look up to idols, and take cues from their journey, but you'll never replicate it because you're an individual. Your sandwich is your own.

But the "Jeremy Fall, Food Guy" train had left the station, and it felt impossible for me to stop it, so I just let myself go with what everyone wanted from me. I went full throttle into the restaurant world, and as I became more established, I found myself being drawn into projects and collaborations that made sense on paper but really didn't fit who I was. At all. These were not my kind of sandwiches.

Meanwhile, my anxiety cough was beginning to flare up, and my thoughts were spiraling more than ever. I love food, but my identity is so much more complex than that. I am a product of the underground, of pop-up culture. I was on the right path, driving on the wrong side of the road. I needed to hit the brakes and figure out how to get back on track. My track.

A solution was born in the kitchen of my good friend Miguel, a Grammy-winning producer and artist. He came to Nighthawk and we talked about how we're both breakfast-for-dinner people, and how he'd had an idea for something a little unusual.

"Dude, I have this idea about making beats in my kitchen and turning it into a show," he said. We paper-clipped my food and his music and came up with *Beats for Breakfast*, our music/cooking show where we serve up weekly food and beats while shooting the shit. It would be several years before the show premiered (on Facebook Watch, if you're interested).

We built a following and got some great press. But even before the accolades and the fans confirmed that we were doing something cool, the idea had served its purpose. It reminded me of who I really am. It reminded me that a successful career is composed of a series of trials and errors, and throughout, we have to keep checking back in, responding to what feels right and what feels wrong, and honoring that. It's a difficult part of the process, and incredibly uncomfortable when you're trying on different identities, and different recipes, trying to figure out which one feels absolutely right. Eventually, though, you'll keep getting closer to the one that's real. And that's the one that will allow you to achieve more than professional success. It'll take you to that magical place called fulfillment.

RX COOKBOOK

My Sarahpist connected me with a woman I'll call Miss Rx, my psychiatrist. I liked her. She didn't have any hard-and-fast solutions and wasn't quick to prescribe. She explained that we'd probably have to explore a bunch of different medications before we found the right one, the right cocktail, but to get there might be a bumpy ride. There was no set recipe for medication, just an approximation we'd tweak as we went along.

She started me off on the most conservative, mildest medication possible. I tried that. It made me so dizzy I nearly fell off a balcony while I was looking for a new apartment. They put me on a medication for bipolar disorder, and I turned into a megalomaniac for a week. If I'd stayed on it much longer I probably would have run for president.

Then I went on a different drug, and she warned me that it might make things feel worse before they got better.

"It might make you gain weight. And you might suffer some serious mood swings at first. And it might not work."

"Okay. Great. Awesome."

"In six weeks, you'll find out."

"Fuck it," I said. It had taken me years to arrive at this point, on the doorstep of psychiatric medication. I saw no point in turning back.

It took about eight weeks to find the right combination and strength of medication. Those were some of the hardest weeks of my life. There

were days when I couldn't get out of bed, where I didn't care if everyone in the world died. I literally gave no fucks.

Then one day, I was in the shower, feeling really bothered by a situation I was going through with a friend of mine. I felt my anxiety creeping back, but different, somehow. It was like I had stepped outside of
myself and could observe the spiraling mechanism in my mind. And
as soon as I did, the spiral began to fade away and instead of obsessing
over how much the situation was stressing me out, I realized that actually, I felt okay. It had passed.

The medication was working. It was progressively rewiring the negative feedback loop in my brain. I started laughing in the shower.

Holy fucking shit. This is me. The real me.

I felt relaxed, aware of my feelings, but not ruled by them. The
anxiety wasn't cluttering my thoughts. Honestly, I had never felt more
like myself than I did in that moment. Had I found a recipe for mental
health? It was too soon to tell, at that point. But something about taking that huge step towards my own kind of healing caused everything
else in my life, including my business, to shift. I could no longer exist
as king of this pile of bullshit I had created. I had to find new ways to
be creative, while remaining completely honest about who I really am.
No fronting.

WHY I HEART DRUGS

One in every five American adults suffers with a mental health condition. Some of these people can function well enough on their own, or
with therapy alone. However, some of us can really benefit from medication management for mental health. I'm not suggesting it as a cure-all,

but I do feel the need to call out the medication misconceptions that are genuinely harmful to people like me, for whom psychiatric medication is imperative. If I hadn't been scared shitless of psych meds, I might have found healing much sooner than I did.

A lot of people worry that they'll become addicted to psychiatric medication, as did I. Addiction runs in my family, and I was desperate to break the mold. Psychiatric medications are not addictive in the same way that recreational and illegal drugs are. They're administered in a controlled and therapeutic dose.

I've never felt myself jonesing for my Lexapro, but I will say this—I'm pretty addicted to the way they make me feel more sober, present, and healthy than ever before.

Another worry I had, before getting prescribed, was that my personality would change. What I found was that my personality remained the same, minus the anxious part, because my neurochemical imbalances were being addressed. In fact, I felt myself restored, and more "Jeremy" than ever before, with the help of these drugs. People around me said the same. That I seemed more relaxed, more able to be myself around them. Wild that a little pill can unlock so much of me that was always there, but drowning under panic attacks and insecurity.

Many people with mental health symptoms avoid taking meds because they worry about being tired all the time, and I did feel sleepy and out of sorts when we were trying to figure out my formula. But once we did, I felt noticeably energized, refreshed. Without the depression that was keeping me in bed, I felt more motivated to move around and do shit like go to the gym.

I started feeling so good on medication, it brought up one of my other concerns—what if I had to stay on this shit forever? The truth is, some people do remain on medication for years, even decades, maybe the rest of their lives. That used to scare me until I realized its lifesaving benefits, for me and so many. I would never question a diabetic's need for insulin, but it's strange that we view medication for our mental health as different somehow, even when it can provide incredible benefits to our health and well-being.

Sometimes I think about what my "unaltered" brain used to be like. It was unhealthy, but for some reason, I believed that getting treatment was a sign of personal weakness, and a lack of courage. But it took all the strength I had for me to seek help. Accepting that I needed medication to manage my mental health was a sign that I had decided to take my health seriously, and it was the bravest choice I'd ever made. I learned that just because I'm on medication, and someone else isn't, it doesn't mean there's something wrong with me. Social comparisons can play such negative roles in mental health management, and just because one person can keep their symptoms at bay without medication, this doesn't mean that solution is best for someone else. Fuck anyone else's recipe for mental health, and find your own path to peace. If anyone judges you for it, don't let it prevent you from continuing to seek help.

That being said, I did feel compelled to bring up the topic of Adderall with my Sarahpist. I mean, so many people are on it—is everyone diagnosed with ADHD now? Or has it become a normalized energy boost, like a cup of coffee (or three). Of course, as someone blessed with Nature's Adderall—aka anxiety disorder and OCD—I've never had a need or a desire to explore this particular branch of Western medicine. But these days, it felt like I was in the minority. Funny how people can be skeptical of SSRIs and other psychiatric medications while happily popping Addies all day, as a way to stay motivated at work or party past their bedtime. What's the deal with that?

"Are you asking me if I think attention deficit disorder exists on the mass scale that it appears to?" said Sarah, for clarification.

"Yeah! Do you think a lot of people who don't actually have ADD get an Adderall prescription nonetheless?"

"It's possible, but it's not that easy to get an Adderall prescription these days. In fact, fewer and fewer pharmacies are stocking it now. It's hard to get, it's not flowing. Which has been really tough for the people who genuinely need it to function."

It's true—I looked it up, and at the time of writing, the FDA had confirmed widespread reports of a significant shortage of the immediate release formulation of amphetamine mixed salts—Adderall—a shortage that may well last for the foreseeable future. Apparently, the drop in supply began due to a labor shortage at Teva, the pharmaceutical company that produces it, causing production delays that began showing up at other companies. Additionally, an increase in ADHD diagnoses has been driving up demand for Adderall in recent years.

Friends had told me they used it to help them complete certain tasks—like packing boxes, cleaning, and paperwork—but that it didn't necessarily aid them creatively, which I thought was interesting.

"So if you don't actually have ADD, it's not necessarily a panacea for creative people," she said. "In fact, it can get in the way of your creativity."

I found myself increasingly fascinated by this world of medications, by the way our culture normalizes certain aspects of being on drugs, while demonizing others. Increasingly, it felt like the only way to venture forward was to do what Sarah had been telling me to do all along, and just listen to my body, observe my thoughts, and slowly, carefully venture along the road to rewiring my anxious mind.

As I walked down my own path to healing, and started feeling more like myself, I noticed myself being drawn to different worlds, different people, and different ways to express my creativity. These new pastures existed outside of the Hollywood scene I'd grown up in, and it wasn't even in the food industry. It was in the world of NFTs—those little non-fungible tokens—that I found myself finally feeling at home. What's cool about NFTs is that they can't be reproduced. There can be only one original. And that's where the value occurs.

As I became more and more involved in the NFT community online, I started to feel like this was the medium that could allow me to take all my life experiences and paper-clip them into something really unique. The world of NFTs existed at the intersection of every-thing that I love—art, honesty, and community. A community where it doesn't matter who you know, or how many followers you have on social media; one that actually rejects the old models of fame and influencer dominance. In the NFT space, you're judged solely on what you bring to the table in terms of knowledge and what you can share.

The way the NFT market functions clicked with me, and I quickly became someone who had something to say about it. It wasn't built on a flex, it wasn't built on me talking my way in, or hyping myself. I learned from the ground up, just like everyone else, and then I created a community of my own, helping artists buy and sell their own NFTs.

Giving back was something I had never really done before. I'd been so obsessed with following other people's recipes to become a different version of myself, I'd ignored the truth in front of me. That as soon as you start following your own recipe, everything flows so easily that you're able to drop the facade. You're able to think about bigger things. Like helping people.

In late 2021, I sent a message out on Twitter that read, "Hey, NFT community. If you don't have food this holiday, let me know and I'll send you money over crypto."

Paying it forward is a basic tenet of NFT life, and I was delighted when people from all over the globe took me up on my offer.

One morning, I received videos from a group of kids in India who were holding bags from Burger King, saying, "Thank you, Jeremy!"

Have it your way.

It was, without doubt, one of my first truly proud moments. The only flex in this community is *not* flexing. The greatest flex is to give back, and to be authentic and communal, not to show up with old status-based attitudes that make inauthentic bullshitters of us all.

In that way, it's the opposite of influencer culture. Whereas Instagram influencers may publicly showcase their fancy dinners or share photos of themselves on trips to Paris or Dubai because the concept of success is about posting constant highlights from your life—and one-upping each of those posts with a better filter to gain more likes and subscribers, to say nothing of getting free trips, clothes, and cosmetics, as a marketer—NFTs and the new modes of thinking on Web3 are attempting to eliminate this kind of toxicity. Maybe part of the reason people have such high hopes for the open-source platforms and decentralized messaging of Web3, the next generation of the internet, is because it echoes our collective desire for greater transparency, accountability, and openness with ourselves.

I was visiting rapper Ty Dolla $ign at his studio one day, and he mentioned that he was interested in buying NFT art. We thought it was a good idea to go live on social media together and ask people to submit their own art. Thousands responded with links to their work on OpenSea, the main NFT marketplace. Ty and I found an artist we liked, and we both bought a piece from the same collection; each piece was linked to the artist's blockchain, meaning it was an original piece of digital art, and priced at around $500 per artwork. Then, we moved on. We thought the art was dope, and that's simply how it started. It reminded me of the days when I worked the velvet rope at Les Deux and would let people in based not on how much money they had, but on whether their energy and style were cool. It just felt right.

A few hours later, the artist, who is based in India, sent me a message.

"Hey, you bought my art. Thank you! It's paying for my father's medical bills," he wrote.

He sent me photos of his father, who was in the hospital and in a coma. I was so moved and wanted to share his story publicly. My social following then began buying his art after learning about him. He and I have since become friends—I check in on him and his father, and he messages me often. We ended up doing a live chat together on Twitter, and he was brought to tears.

"You changed my life," he said. "And now all I want to do is help someone else like you helped me."

An incredible exchange like this had never happened to me. Not in everyday life, because I don't typically find myself walking around the streets of India, and heading into someone's home to buy their art. Sure, I frequent galleries, but how many artists from small villages around the globe have the ability to access the art world *and* have collectors even see their work? Everyday artists can't get their work in those galleries, and my new friend in India certainly couldn't have.

Before becoming involved in the NFT community, the worlds I had been existing in were largely based on hype and exclusivity—nightlife, restaurants, food TV. It is hard to penetrate those worlds, and most people who do end up there have to lie about themselves to gain access, fake it till you make it, just like I did. You might even connect with a large audience, but if you're not following your own recipe, you can end up feeling very lonely, depressed, and anxious, because you're not genuinely interacting with the world. With NFTs, though, the opportunity is in flipping the script. To present a public face that felt more like the person I really am. What a huge fucking relief.

Every day, I connect with my followers on Twitter by beginning with a "Good morning" and ending with a "Goodnight." The entire community does it; we act as a family—one that doesn't judge or require you to get past a velvet rope. It's a world where, instead of success, honesty and authenticity are the influencers. People don't care if you're already successful; they care if you have a good story that's not about trips to Dubai or Christian Dior dresses.

In the NFT world, everything that once triggered my constant sense of being an imposter is muted. I can't pretend to know people or have more cryptocurrency than I really do, because that information is accessible to anyone. Every single transaction is recorded in public—there's no flexing there. Yes, I came in as someone who's a public figure, but that bought me zero authority in the space. I had to rebuild myself from scratch. Just like everyone else did, including prominent basketball stars like Shaquille O'Neal. No one, including me, has been doing it for long, so there are no experts. Everyone has to write their own recipe, and forge ahead on their own path through this brave new world. So now I'm seeing my success as it's being built, and this time, it feels real.

Of course, the future is unclear with NFTs, as it is with anything. How long will this community be about leveling the playing field, and make me feel better about myself as a business person and a creative? I don't know. How do we actually maintain a society where we're allowed to be who we are and also wear our hearts on our sleeves without being punished for it?

It's confusing and scary, but at least my voice—Jeremy's voice—is rising above all the noise because I've learned to listen to my feelings. I've learned that emptiness is *not* what keeps us afloat.

These days, I am still known in the food space as a chef, a restaurateur. Celebrities might have an idea for a project in the food and beverage world, and they'll talk to their manager, who'll say, "We should talk to Jeremy Fall, the Food Guy." But when people ask me what I do, what category I stand in, I tell them I don't know. I'm just . . . me.

I'm creating things out of nothing, myself included, and that's the only real recipe I can stand by. I can tell you the things I've learned, I can share my tools like paper-clipping, and the Studio 54 formula, like authenticity as an antidote for imposter syndrome and Lexapro for acute anxiety disorder—but I can't tell you how to make them your own. That part is up to you, and it involves detaching from tried and tested ideas.

From boring mass-market films to chain stores that lack soul, outdated myths about psychiatric medication, and restaurants that are trying to recreate something that felt fresh five years ago—recipes are unhealthy and can lead to creative and psychological unease. Following other people's recipes is how we can so easily attach our careers, our identity, our mental health to other people's opinions and expectations—and that's when the illness begins.

There are no "right" ways to be happy and successful other than the ones your intuition is pulling you towards. No recipes. Fuck your recipe. Because if you follow someone else's, all you'll wind up with is one hell of an inauthentic burrito.

5

PURSE HOOKS, LIGHTING, AND ANXIOUS IMPERFECTION

Mental Instability as a Superpower

LIKE THIS QUOTE FROM DESIGNERS AND ARCHITECTS CHARLES AND RAY EAMES:

The details are not the details, they make the product just like the details make the architecture. The gauge of the wire, the selection of the wood, the finish of the castings—the connections, the connections, the connections. It will be in the end these details that provide service to the customers, and give the product its life.

I don't know much about the Eameses' state of mind, but I can totally relate. It's an obsessive attention to detail that creates identity, and tells a story. Details make the difference between what's good and what's best. Creativity contains within it aspects of obsession that have all the traits of mental illness, until you see the beautiful results. Without some obsession, you're probably performing well enough, rather than as well as you possibly can.

But what's the difference between a healthy attention to detail, and an obsessiveness that actually gets in the way? The line between them is sometimes thin. All I know is that my brain never stops, and that's what helped me get ahead, what helped me look at the world in a unique and hyper-curated way.

My anxiety is rooted in the fear of the unknown.

My anxiety is trying to prepare myself for every possible outcome, which no one can actually do—especially not in the restaurant business. But I tried.

Every time I opened a bar or restaurant, I obsessively curated all aspects of the whole experience, anticipating every possible scenario that could happen when a customer was there. That's my anxious mind, working for, not against me. It does that sometimes. My mental illness manifests as hyper-attention to human reactions, and it's my superpower, depending on how I choose to harness it.

In her book *Good Anxiety: Harnessing the Power of the Most Misunderstood Emotion*, professor of neuroscience and psychology Wendy Suzuki outlines strategies to turn anxiety into something productive. Anxiety, she says, is trying to give us information about what we appreciate and what we value in our lives. She wants us to make friends with our anxiety and reap all the gifts it can offer.

I suppose she's right, to some degree.

ANXIETY IS WHY I fix everything before it breaks.

Anxiety is why I plan people's emotional experiences before they happen.

Anxiety is why I overthink like it's an Olympic sport.

"There is a gift of productivity that comes from anxiety," Suzuki told NPR. "So often anxiety kind of shuts us down—we can't focus. However, here is a gift that can come from your anxiety, and that is that 'what if' list that comes with your anxiety. What if I don't know the answer? What if they ask me about this part of the book and I can't remember the study? Everybody can turn your 'what if' list into a to-do list. It's satisfying because, again, going back to evolution, our stress response and the anxiety response evolved to be resolved with an action. Our stress is getting our muscles active to do something to take some action."

I envy people who work eight hours a day, and then . . . stop. But when you have anxiety like I do, you're on the clock, all the time.

You're working in the shower.

You're working in the car.

You're thinking about things like light bulbs and purse hooks when you should be relaxing or having fun, but it's okay because purse hooks, by the way, are the shit.

Purse hooks secure your handbag or purse to a table, bar, or bathroom door, which is crucial because a Birkin placed on the floor is just wrong, and will collect all manner of gross bacteria. Did you know that the bottom of a woman's purse ranks number seven on the list of the germiest places in everyday life, according to some geniuses on the *Today* show? You do now. Welcome to my germophobic world.

Purse hooks have been around since the 1920s, but they weren't huge in the Hollywood bar and nightlife scene I inhabited in the 2000s, even with the rise of the statement purse. Who wants to put their beautiful statement purse on the floor? Not my clientele, and some of them were even starting to bring their own hooks to bars and clubs. That's why I became one of the first people in town to absolutely fucking insist on purse hooks under tables, and some days I would spend hours thinking, obsessing on those things.

Did I want an original L-style hook with a circular pad and a rigid bent wire, or an S-shaped purse hanger? How about a spring-closing bracelet type of purse hook? How low should the damn hook go? What would happen if the purse strap was thicker than usual, or if there were two bags needing to go on that fucking hook, WHAT THEN?

But that's how the anxiety goes. Every little detail, obsessively considered. Which is a big part of what made me good at my job. Obsessive-compulsive disorder is a secondary diagnosis of mine, an aspect of my anxiety disorder. Though the tone of the cultural discussion about mental health—especially that encircling anxiety and depression—has become more accepting of late, society's understanding of OCD has lagged behind.

What we do know is this—many people with OCD have an overactive imagination, as kids and adults. And while that can benefit anyone trying to be creative and think outside the box, it also brings with it a lot of irrational thoughts and fears. It means that a lot of the time, I'm worrying about some unknown future and what catastrophes can happen, instead of actually experiencing the moment that's happening. But at least the customers are happy. At least their purses are safe and nowhere near the floor.

Being a detail-obsessed OCD people-pleaser with codependency issues and imposter syndrome, I took my psychological lemons and turned them into lemonade. I love giving customers special moments that are so memorable they want to come back. The part of me that feels worthless, the part where Bob lives, thrives on the external validation. Every day as a restaurateur, I'm auditioning to take space in people's minds in the hopes that they will say, "Yes, Jeremy, you ARE the best." That's the ultimate reward because one of my deepest fears is that I'll disappoint people. It's an aspect of my mental illness that really blooms in a food and beverage setting.

Here are some more things that keep me up at night when I'm launching a restaurant.

Height of seating. Where the table hits. Silverware, glassware, candles, black napkins because the white ones lint, and even lint-free ones still lint. The acoustics have to be good so there's a vibe, but the music's not so loud that people can't hear each other.

Music should have a beat, but nothing too fast—it has to keep your energy up but not make you turn up. This, of course, is why I curate every playlist myself (aside from when I had Robin Thicke collab on one of my playlists—other than that it's me).

Front of house should say "right this way" instead of "follow me."

Pulling out chairs for people—that's important. I think pulling out chairs for people is a nice thing to do and makes people feel special.

Smells, even nice ones, are an absolute no. No scented candles. They'll detract from the food.

Flowers, only if they are devoid of fragrance.

Bathroom lighting should be moody—who wants to see their zits and lines in between courses? But it should be bright enough for women to be able to do makeup touchups.

The font of the menu is important, as is the color of the font, and how the lighting bounces off the words.

Don't even get me started on light bulbs. The lights in my venues are always yellow-tinged because white lights are fucking death and feel like hospitals. You don't want lights to be orange, but amber is good. All my light bulbs are amber, and as much as I joke about Edison bulbs being overused as fuck, at least they're the right color. In conclusion, may I recommend bulbs in "warm white," a white light with a hint of yellow candlelight, always 3,000 K or below? Warm lights make a space feel smaller, intimate, and more comfortable. It dulls shades of blue while enhancing reds and oranges, and adds a yellow tint to whites and greens. This affects the way the customer sees their food, of course. Light bulbs allowed me to be in control of how my customers saw what they were putting in their bodies, and I carried that responsibility like the weight of the world on my shoulders.

I require a very specific level of ambient lighting throughout, using chandeliers, ceiling or wall-mount fixtures, track lighting, and/or recessed lights, then I think about task lighting, how we can enhance visual clarity and prevent eyestrain, and blend it with accent lighting to draw attention to unique features that I want to highlight.

A curated light show, designed by Me and My Anxiety™.

THE POWER OF BROKE

Every rent day. Every bill day. Every time I buy a big-ticket item, my scarcity anxiety is activated, and I remember that nothing is permanent. Love, money, health, even life itself, can all vanish overnight.

I never thought Jared would die young—but he did.

I never thought my anxiety would bring me close to the edge of sanity and threaten my business and all my relationships—but it did.

Scarcity anxiety is an aspect of my mental illness that has never gone away, and it shows up for me every month, when my bills come out of my account. That's when the panic sets in. I'm talking a sense of complete doom and gloom, end of days shit. This fear that tomorrow it could all be gone.

I am broke.

I have no more money.

Soon, I'll be homeless.

That kind of thing.

I have chosen to exist in a roller-coaster business environment, after all. But that monthly terror is not a bad thing. I hope I never lose that fear of being broke.

The Power of Broke is a book by Daymond John and Daniel Paisner, and it posits that being broke, financially, is not an entrepreneurial death sentence so long as you use it as fuel to think outside the box and take risks that people with money are too scared, or complacent, to take.

Daymond John was a founder of FUBU, short for "for us, by us," one of the first fashion brands targeted at the Black community. He started it in the '90s without knowing how to draw and only being able to stitch a straight line. The company's worth grew to $6 billion, but it started on forty dollars that Daymond used to buy some cotton and cloth, and knit an overpriced but cool hat he'd seen. He sold eighty hats for ten dollars apiece, and crashed his car while counting his money at the wheel. Still, he pushed on with his endeavors, and that's the core message of his book.

If you have no money, you'll automatically find resources others don't look for. When you're broke, you're looking for opportunity where other people see only problems. Brokeness forces you to apply whatever you've got, leading you to use resources in new, creative ways other people don't see.

You don't need money to make money. All you need is hunger. A form of scarcity anxiety. The trick is maintaining that good anxiety, even when your bank balance tells you it's time to chill and take a vacation.

Steve Jobs sold his car to fund the first few products Apple made.

Michael Dell didn't know computers well, so he designed one for amateurs like himself.

Our society places so much emphasis on wealth and status that when you have little or no money, it can feel utterly dehumanizing, because our financial status has been so deeply tied up with notions of self-worth. We've been conditioned all our lives to believe that money is the only true measure of our success, and even though (spoiler alert) it isn't, it's hard to undo the social conditioning.

When you grow up broke, it's hard to believe you'll never be there again. Why do you think immigrants and minorities often work harder than everyone else? It's because we know how easy it is to be left behind. To fall through the cracks. We've seen the dark side of capitalism, the promises of an American Dream that suckers people into minimum wage jobs and keeps us there. But the experience of being without can be one of the greatest motivational tools on earth.

Being broke can spark fires in you, a hunger for change.

Scarcity anxiety can act like a career defibrillator; it kick-starts your heart, gets you motivated, and it can push you closer to your goals.

So every month, I take that dread and use it. I look at the worst-case scenarios swirling around my head and pretend I'm already in them, then I make a plan of action.

Everything's fucked—so now what?

What do I need to do to make back the money?

How am I going to survive?

Usually, the result is I wind up coming up with a shitload of ideas. Some of them forgettable, some of them great.

No matter where you are in your life and career, keep hold of that energy, that panic, that desire for more. Remember, good anxiety can take you places. Broke can arouse your creative spirit, enliven the impetus to make changes. Even if you're not broke anymore, it's good to tap into that energy on a fairly regular basis. Broke keeps you in check. Broke keeps you grateful.

Maintain the mindset that nothing is real and everything could be taken away at a moment's notice, and tap into your sense of purpose and energy in a useful way. Maintain your hunger throughout your life and career, as part of your practice.

I'm not broke anymore. But when I tell myself that in the end, I really have nothing other than my desire to be more, it lights a fresh fire under me. Gets me moving and thinking creatively. I invite you to allow a sense of impermanence and insecurity to walk alongside you— not leading the way, but there as friends and reminders. As fuel for your good anxiety. The kind that will always push you to the next level of your potential, no matter how much money you have in the bank.

My dad called me the other day.

"You'll never believe this," he said. "I went to Sprouts, and it was $1.50 for a pound of tomatoes! Then I remembered at Super King— well, guess how much a pound of tomatoes costs there?"

He usually likes to call at the absolute busiest moment in my day.

"Dad, I don't fucking care. A dollar?"

"*Fifty cents* at Super King. So I left Sprouts, went to Super King, and bought a pound of tomatoes."

"So you saved a dollar."

"Yup."

"Dad, how much did it cost you in gas to drive to Super King?"

"I don't know."

"I guarantee it was more than a dollar. Also, don't you think you're better off buying higher-quality vegetables that will last you a week, instead of discounted ones that will last a couple of days?"

"Jeremy! I am NOT paying top dollar for a pound of tomatoes!"

"So did you eat all your tomatoes before they went bad?"

"Yes. I made a big salad, and a gazpacho. Now I have a stomach-ache. Or maybe it's a heart attack, I don't know."

There's a big difference between the awareness that money is ephemeral and can be taken from you (scarcity anxiety), and a fear-based frugality that will actually COST you money in the end (scarcity mentality).

Scarcity anxiety can push you forward and fuel creativity.

Scarcity mentality will hold you back and make you save pennies while losing dollars.

"By the way, I want to move to Joshua Tree," my dad added.

Joshua Tree is a small, bohemian desert town about two hours east of LA. You've seen it on every influencer's social media, at some point. Girls in white lace dresses with beige fedoras and Celine sunglasses posing in front of those distinctive, gnarled trees.

"Why? Are you going to become an influencer?"

"No, but Joshua Tree has all my favorite stores. There's a Marshalls, a 99-cent Store, a Dollar Tree."

"Dad, how much is it going to cost you to uproot your life in LA so you can be closer to the Dollar Tree?"

"Maybe there's a Dollar Tree in LA."

"There is definitely a Dollar Tree in LA."

My father operates from the mindset that saving a few cents FEELS better, even if it costs him money in the long term. A scarcity mentality has cost my father time, possibly his health, and has definitely inspired some interesting decisions on his part, because he doesn't see the crucial difference between being frugal and being a chronic under-spender. A frugal person makes sure their spending matches their financial goals; a chronic under-spender is so afraid of spending money, they'll avoid spending any even at the cost of personal and financial well-being.

Under-spending is frugality taken to extremes, and at the root of it is fear. My dad was scared because he'd gone through the same things I had. Because he'd lived the Studio 54 lifestyle only for it to be gone, in a flash. Because he'd watched my mother and me struggle, and been unable to help. His anxiety, untreated and unharnessed, was manifesting as a sort of paralysis.

Part of me wished I could connect my dad with my Sarahpist, but he laughed out loud when I suggested it.

"I'm saving money on groceries so you now want me to get therapy?"

"No! I'm saying you're an under-spender and it's having an impact on your happiness," I said.

"I feel great."

"Are you sure?"

"Yep!"

Sometimes, we learn to rationalize our toxic behaviors. We are similar, my father and I.

JUST A NUMBER

One night, I had dinner with my close friend Chris Knight, a music executive. I was looking for a manager and wanted his feedback on my options. If I had to be the Food Guy, I wanted to be the one who operated beyond food. I wanted to be the Food Guy who understands culture and art. I had already ditched all my food PR and gotten music PR people instead. No, I'm not a musician, but I'm obsessed with music and I think in terms of music production when I'm conceiving ideas for food. Call it a form of mental paper-clipping, if you will. Getting a music publicist would enable me to step outside of the tried-and-tested route of existing solely in the food press and open my world up to media that were interested in culture as a whole.

Chris listened as I explained my goals, how I wanted to be part of a cultural conversation that extended beyond the local foodie scene.

"Hey, man, can we throw our name in the hat?" he asked. I was surprised—he had just started working with Roc Nation, Jay-Z's management arm. Was he saying he wanted to manage me himself?

"Yeah, of course! I would love that!"

"Alright, let's see if I can get approval from the rest of the company," he said, and within a few weeks, I signed with Roc Nation as a Food Guy who wanted to break walls down, blend comfort and luxury, and mix genres to create paper-clipped Studio 54 ideas that were greater than the sum of their parts. All this with a 520 credit score and no credit cards to my name.

Like so many kids in America, my credit was destroyed after I took out student loans, $14,000 worth, which had gone into collections, and which I had ignored my whole life. Since then, I'd lived a cash lifestyle. Even when I was cooking on national TV and opening restaurants all over the country, I had almost zero purchasing power. When I bought my first car, a Prius, I had to have my mom cosign because I had a credit score of 520. That's considered Very Poor by the good folks at FICO, and almost certainly too low to get me a mortgage or a car or anything consumer society values. Nonetheless, I didn't give a shit.

Why would I? Life was unfolding exactly according to plan. I had risen above the odds and become a "Food Guy" (even though I wasn't really a Food Guy), and I was running with it because I had cash in hand.

Credit scores were these laughable, cruel metrics, in my opinion. They offered such an inadequate representation of who I was, how hard I'd worked, the difficulties of my childhood that I had overcome. A credit score is just a fucking number designed to control us, and communicate my worth to a society that never really cared about me in the first place. But after a while, I came to the conclusion that I would eventually have to move out of a cash lifestyle, and found a credit fixer to help. Surely it couldn't be that hard. I knew I could pay off the $14,000, after all.

"Fine, but they're not going to remove it off your credit immediately," the credit fixer told me. "In fact, TransUnion takes eight years to update. We're going to have to fight to make your credit score reflect your reality."

My rampant imposter syndrome and anxiety kicked into gear. I felt that familiar sense of outrage and injustice. This metric's reliability was off! The system we live in is set up to disadvantage those who grew up broke, and it made me mad as hell! My anxiety morphed into something that felt like righteous anger, and a desire to prove the world wrong. Because oftentimes, the world *is* wrong. America may rank relatively high when it comes to so-called "Opportunity"—read, the American Dream—but who really has access to that dream? And why were there so many barriers to entry?

I was still on a credit score of 520, driving a used Prius cosigned by my mom, and living in a grungy studio apartment in Hollywood, but I knew none of those things were measures of my true potential, or worth. I harnessed that outrage and turned it into success, and so can anyone. The greater the outrage, the brighter the fires you can start in this world. I started some fires and burned down my past identity, self-soothing by embracing a luxury lifestyle that was the opposite of my roots.

I bought the all-black Rolex Submariner and the Cartier bracelet when my company J. Fall Group got acquired in 2019 by a company called K2. The history of Rolex watches is one of my passions. I can tell you how old one is on sight, as well as its probable history. As for the Cartier bracelets . . . it's a millennial status thing. They've been around since 1969, when Italian designer Aldo Cipullo (who'd built his reputation at Tiffany & Co.) took a job at Cartier and came up with an idea to sell his chastity belt–inspired cuffs only to couples, including Robert Evans and Ali MacGraw, Dyan Cannon and Cary Grant, and Richard Burton and Elizabeth Taylor. I love them because they're like handcuffs. Impossible to take off, which makes me feel safe.

The oval-shaped bracelets are held together by two grub screws that, when tightened, lock onto the wearer's wrist. They're meant "to sanctify inseparable love." Costing anywhere from $4,500 to $56,500, they also signify a high income. Some hospital emergency rooms in New York keep a tiny Cartier Love screwdriver on hand in case a high net worth individual gets wheeled in on a gurney, wearing an impossible-to-remove Cartier bracelet.

Luxury was always something I wanted for myself, because it placed Band-Aids over my fundamental lack of self-worth. That's the dynamic of the luxury industry, and that's why products made for relatively little in factories in Italy sell for thousands of dollars when branded for sale in luxury marketplaces.

"You with your Louis Vuitton wallet!" my dad would say, embarrassed when I pulled it out at dinner to pay the bill.

Then he'd glance at my shoes and say, "How much did you pay for those sneakers?"

"Dad, my wallet cost me $450, and I'll keep it for ten years minimum. That's forty-five dollars a year. Less than a Netflix subscription."

"Don't be ridiculous."

"The sneakers cost me $350. I'll have them for two years, and they'll carry me from meeting to work session and everywhere in between for . . . about fifty cents a day. I'm okay with that too. I can't afford to NOT buy quality because cheap products are the worst investment you can make."

My dad will never understand why I buy $300 sweatpants, even though I'm going to wear the shit out of them for years. Or why I'll buy the $300 Christmas tree that will last me a decade. In the end, my father and I probably spend the same amount of money on accessories and shoes, because I'll buy high-quality goods less frequently and he'll buy the shit out of some Payless shoes that won't last him the year.

But yes . . . the Cartier bracelets are extra.

Acquiring wealth and the symbols associated with high net worth is a method of self-soothing, of finding calm amid the anxiety that exists within me. Some days it feels like a Cartier cuff really could bridge the gap between hope and hopelessness, but so does a fancy dessert, or a message of support from a stranger on social media. External indicators that convey safety and security offer temporary sanctuary within the storm of everyday life, and the neuroses that I developed over time. But the trophies I've acquired have, ironically, fed into a projection of myself that is rooted in inauthenticity. That's why there are lingering, incorrect perceptions of me that I'm still fighting to dispel. That I'm a trust funder. A Hollywood rich kid, when the truth is, it was my broke mindset that made me rich.

There was a time when I had no guarantee of escaping my probable destiny, and I've never felt so supported. People in my industry rooted for me back when I was nobody, because everybody loves an underdog. I was just some twenty-three-year-old, trying to make it, opening his first bar, and it felt like the whole city had my back. I was underground, a rookie who came from nowhere, a baby with nothing to lose. A dreamer, with everything to prove, *because* he is broke.

Whether you're broke in resources, or broke in knowledge, there are two paths you can take. One can keep you in the same place, depressed. The other path can lead you into a primal survival state that kick-starts you into your most creative self. An anxious state that overrides self-doubt and turns you into the proverbial Fool, stepping over the cliff before realizing you can fly. When you're on the edge, the stakes are high, the struggle is authentic, and your hunger is real. Think like you don't have a safety net or a backup plan. Imagine failure is no longer an option, and see what happens.

Today, my ideation processes are calm, organized, and streamlined. I know what questions to ask myself, and how high or low to hang the purse hooks.

Can I execute this?

Is it scalable?

Will my team think this is on brand?

How will this fit on my Instagram?

Can I correlate this with something else in my business narrative?

How do we handle trademarks and branding?

And so on.

Still, I fight for that urgency that got me started in life. That fire.

Broke can be an empowered place to be in your life, even if it's a place you're desperately trying to escape. And when you do escape it, in hindsight, you may wish to continue to appreciate the unique and energetic power of broke. The reaction it elicits from people, the sheer momentum it is capable of building. The negative space that begs to be filled, the blank canvas that compels you to make your mark on the world.

It's common to lose that creative fire as you master the logistics of running your life and career and business. But each time you do, remind yourself to inject a little bit of "fuck it" into your process. Go for broke. Enter that deeply creative state, and let the story write itself. If you get too sure and comfortable in your ways, don't be afraid to doubt yourself every once in a while, rethink what you know, and remember where you came from. When your dreams were just that—thoughts in the ether, waiting for you to give them form.

ANXIETY SAVES!

"Sarah, what's the difference between healthy attention to detail and obsessiveness that actually gets in the way? And what if you're sort of treading the line between both?"

"You know," she said, "if whatever OCD thing you're doing is not a problem for you, if it's not a functional impairment, then cool. But if it's starting to get in the way of your life and dysfunction is happening, like you're not able to get places on time, you're micromanaging other people, you're creating chaos, you're creating problems, et cetera, it's a problem in your life, then that's where we get into territory where it's unhealthy. But if your relationships, friendships, and work life are not being negatively impacted by your OCD behaviors, then there's no real need to alter them. Especially not if they're working for you."

I had just found out that good stress is sometimes referred to as "eustress," meaning stress that leads to a positive response. Eustress is the opposite of distress in that it tends to be short-term and often feels exciting. It's manageable and keeps us motivated and excited about life. Eustress is the silver lining of anxiety. You might feel it during major life transitions like starting a new job, falling in love, and having a kid. Even the excitement of a roller-coaster ride or a first date can bring on this kind of stress.

Eustress is cool.

Eustress is the fluffy kind of anxiety.

But even the spiky, non-eustressy anxiety may be good.

There's anxiety as an early warning system. Maybe it's time to make some changes in your life. Maybe some areas of your life are off track and need adjusting, like a relationship that is no longer working, or a job that's bumming you out. This is the kind of anxiety that contains messages and information on possible adjustments you may need to make in your life. Noticing those anxieties can be a gateway to discovering what we truly value. We feel anxious when we see someone being bullied or harmed, or when a person says something that seems dishonest. Anxiety can act as a radar, showing us the truth.

There's anxiety as a competitive tool. Research has shown that students and athletes who experience anxiety actually display improved performance on tests or while participating in competitive sports. Anxiety can help you push yourself to your limit of achievement. The downside, of course, is when you constantly worry about not being good enough, or you work so hard you don't take time to rest. Anxious overachievers might have difficulty saying no, completing tasks to their liking, or knowing which tasks to prioritize. We might have issues trusting or working with others. These are all things to work on overcoming, if we truly want to harness our anxiety superpower.

There's anxiety that just makes you a better person. People who have experienced anxiety tend to be more empathetic and understanding of the issues that others face. Having gone through personal struggles yourself is the quickest way to become more sensitive and accepting of others. People with anxiety tend to be more concerned about making others feel safe.

People with anxiety can actually make great leaders, as we're always carefully considering multiple outcomes—we've already thought about everything that could go wrong, which makes us great decision-makers and problem-solvers. We're amazing researchers, critical thinkers, and analyzers, and we tend toward higher-level intellectual processing, which can teach us to be smarter as we're constantly exploring ways to solve problems.

In a nutshell, anxiety is fucking awesome.

To a certain extent.

Until the negative pressures of anxiety rob you of focus, calm, and fulfillment, of course. But if you don't let that happen, or if you treat it when it does, anxiety can be the friend you never knew you had. The friend that shows you what your body and mind are able to achieve, even under great pressure. The friend that believes so much in you, you eventually start to believe in yourself.

6

CHICKEN AND BISCUITS >

Channeling the Power of Simplicity

HERE'S THE RECIPE FOR MY EXPERIMENTAL PASTRAMI AGNOLOTTI, INGREDIENTS as follows:

House-made caraway pasta
Short rib pastrami
Mustard brodo (a type of broth)
Red cabbage sauerkraut
Confit fennel
Parmesan

Basically it's a Reuben sandwich in a pasta; we developed it especially for my restaurant Mixtape.

"Mixtape will open in the Fairfax District on Tuesday," said the *LA Times*. "The 140-seat restaurant comes from Jeremy Fall, the 28-year-old restaurateur who opened Nighthawk Breakfast Bar in Hollywood and Marina del Rey, Golden Box in Hollywood and Easy's in Chinatown and Beverly Center. Fall is managed by Roc Nation, the entertainment group founded by Jay-Z. He is the first person from the restaurant industry signed to the company's management roster. 'I really wanted to make this project weird and different,' said Fall."

Hence the agnolotti. It was weird and different, which made me happy.

"Art includes an original sketch by Quincy Jones, a photo collage from rapper Vic Mensa and a painting by Incubus singer Brandon Boyd as well as entries from Tokimonsta, Serj Tankian and Jaden Smith. Anaheim-raised rapper Phora, who recently opened a boutique called Yours Truly on Fairfax, collaborated with Fall on the staff uniforms. Singer Robin Thicke has signed out to create playlists for Mixtape's weekend brunch service."

Mixtape was a whole new dining experience. You ordered cocktails based on your moods, with options including Confident (cognac, spiced pear liqueur, clover honey syrup, and lemon with a cinnamon salt sugar rim) or Pensive (gin, sparkling wine, basil-infused sugar water, and lime). Each drink came with the right to add a song to the night's playlist, and customers could "mix it up" and order a meal on shuffle, meaning the kitchen would choose a dope selection of dishes for them.

"The menu draws upon Fall's combined Tunisian, Caribbean, Jewish and French heritage. Dishes include *merguez* meatballs with *harissa* yogurt, pistachio *dukkah* and *zhoug* oil; smoked salmon with *cacio e pepe* latkes and *gribiche*; fried jerk chicken sandwiches with lemongrass aioli slaw; cauliflower steak with red coconut curry; and caraway agno-lotti with short rib pastrami and mustard brodo."

I was so happy they mentioned the agnolotti. Of course, no one ever ordered the fucking agnolotti. Maybe 2 percent of customers. Mostly, people wanted the chicken sandwich. And I cannot tell you how much that pissed me off, at first.

Supreme. A white T-shirt with a red logo box. That's what blew them up. They rubbed the two sticks, the right way. Arthur Fry and Spencer Silver, creators of Post-it Notes. Paper that you stick to shit. Thirty billion dollars in annual sales. How many Snuggies have been sold? Around thirty million, at fifteen dollars apiece. Do the math.

It took me a long time to actually respect the power of basic, until I realized that accessibility really is the foundation of many a success story, including my own.

I am the paper clip. I am the egg man. I am the glittery remnants of Studio 54. Anything less than high concept feels like a sellout, to me, and one day, I WILL open my fine dining joint that has no tables or chairs, or where every item on the menu contains some form of egg. Maybe. But, for now, the biggest seller on my menu is still the chicken. Chicken and biscuits, chicken alfredo, fried chicken sandwiches, anything—so long as it's chicken. Chicken works, because chicken is what the people want.

Panem et circenses, a Roman guy once said. Bread and circuses. That's how you keep humans happy. In the twenty-first century, we've swapped bread and circuses for chicken and hip hop because that's what America is all about. Basic, universal, and simple, with perfect execution if you want to stand out. Chicken and biscuits means you don't have to reinvent the wheel. Chicken and biscuits means it's okay to "sell out," so long as you do it right, because chicken might just be the thing that allows you to explore all your other weird, Willy Wonka shit, and still pay the bills.

I developed a chicken and biscuits dish that was extra special, if I do say so myself. I used free-range chicken, aged cheddar, and chive biscuits with maple bacon sausage gravy. All quality, everything made from scratch, and fresh. There are a million ways to make chicken and biscuits on the cheap, but if I'm doing basic, I'm doing it with no expense spared. Still, for all the high-end ingredients and attention to detail, there's clearly nothing groundbreaking about it. No epic creative breakthroughs, and for a long time, I felt uncomfortable with that. It irritated me that the least inventive dish on my menu was always the biggest seller.

What did that say about me?

What did people think?

Was I less or more cool now that my businesses were making money?

I had no idea so I asked myself, as I often do, *what would Andy Warhol think?*

Warhol became an icon on the back of a can of Campbell's soup. He didn't judge society for being basic, he celebrated it and became the most iconic artist of his era. I'm not an iconic artist (unless you're talking to my mother), but simple and popular was paying off for me too. So why did I feel so weird about it?

SELL OUT, BUT MAKE IT TOP-SHELF

In any capitalist system, it's difficult to survive as a full-time artist or creative. Artists need to be industrious in order to make a living from art, and they may choose to work with mainstream or government organizations or corporations to supplement their income. It's the "artist's dilemma"—how do you cooperate with large entities while ensuring moral ground? What constitutes "selling out," arguably the worst insult that can be hurled at an artist?

Many people in creative industries are torn between the desire to make an impact on a large scale, and remain true to their artistry. The fear of being too mainstream has kept many an artist trapped in low-paying underground scenes, forced to take on side hustles to pay the bills. How can we "sell out" and still be authentic? Is it possible to be basic AF and maintain integrity? How can we distinguish between the chicken that's good for you, and the chicken that's just . . . pink slime?

Shepard Fairey, known for his iconic OBEY posters, is one of the world's most renowned street artists. But along with his work on the streets, he runs a thriving graphic design business based in Echo Park that caters to big corporations, including Nike and Saks Fifth Avenue. This is his chicken and biscuits work that enables him to wheat paste anti-war slogans on street corners the world over. Fairey is aware of the questionable moral agendas of some of the corporations that commission him, but he still takes their money because it helps fund the projects that are closest to his heart.

"I'm doing things on my own terms outside of the system when necessary, while also seizing opportunities to infiltrate the system and use its machinery to spread my art and ideas, hoping to change the system for the better in the process," he says, assuming the role of Robin Hood, taking from rich corporations and using the money to finance street art that attacks them. Is he authentically selling out, then? Is that what's happening?

The desire for authenticity is a powerful social force, and one that is particularly pervasive in the creative industry. Artists, writers, and designers are expected to find their own voice if they're to stand out within an already crowded field. There is an intense focus on the integrity of creation, and our natural impulse is to seek the reassurance of an authentic truth. When someone is all chicken and biscuits, we feel like financial interest has trumped their artistic integrity, and their personal truth has been lost in the process, because a sellout is someone who has let go of who they really are. Or have they?

There's a snobbery that pours shame on those in the creative fields who express interest in scaling up or boosting their earning power by stepping outside of their niche. And the more I thought about it, me criticizing myself for my own chicken and biscuits was an absurdly elitist, masochistic act. Very few people can afford to turn down branded partnerships or sponsored projects. Not everyone has the luxury of choice. There is a value judgment that is frequently placed on "selling out," but it is laden with privilege that cannot be earned through hard work alone. That's when I realized that I had to let go of my anxiety surrounding the way people perceived my chicken and biscuits. After all, most people are immediately accused of selling out the moment they achieve success. But making money is not selling out—doing something that's not authentic to you, just for money, is selling out. Not being able to pay your bills because you *didn't* do the commercial thing that one time because you were worried what your "cool" friends might think? Now that hurts. I was broke long enough to realize that, actually, there's nothing cooler than being able to support yourself.

To a creative person who values integrity and is worried about the way they're perceived, incorporating chicken and biscuits into their plan can feel like the greatest risk they've ever taken. But it is possible to move between the two worlds—commercial and artistic—and not compromise your authenticity.

The Weeknd wore a red suit for a year because he was playing a character whose storyline concluded on the Super Bowl, directly after which he announced that the character had died. He put $7 million of his own money into it, just because he wanted to. The project perfectly straddled mainstream and cool. And there was nothing basic about it.

The words "revolution" and "movement" have been used to describe NFT technology, which allows for the ownership—and, therefore, the commodification—of digital objects. To those of us who are passionate about NFTs, we see it as a celebration of the intersection of art and technology. But even now, the movement is viewed with suspicion and disdain, with critics asking, "Is this real art, or is this pixelated monkey just another way for people to make money?"

BASIC IS KING

Because everyone was ordering the chicken, it actually made me double down on my creativity. I came up with less and less commercially viable ideas to counterbalance the chicken. How about I partner with an artist on a whole album release of music that plays and syncs with food, so we can explore the way sound waves affect taste? So much paper-clipping, so much juxtaposition, it's getting me hyped just remembering it, even though that shit will never work on a grand scale, and never go beyond a limited pop-up, because it isn't chicken.

As artists, innovators, and creative business people, we really want to peacock. We want to present the world with our wonderful, innovative ideas that are going to save the planet and earn us a shitload of money along the way. We can't help it. We have these big, planet-sized egos—I'm a Leo, by the way—and we're happiest when our ideas are being talked about, worshipped as the freshest, most original, and unique things ever, just like us. But if I opened a Pastrami Agnolotti restaurant, I bet it would bomb in a week.

What's your core product? What's the thing you're trying to share with the world? Is it your fashion? Is it a taco? Can you paper-clip it to something, and create something new that feels different and exciting? Make a fashion taco? Sure, but make sure there's a solid foundation for your innovation. A regular, delicious taco that's paying the bills while you try to figure out how to monetize a $100 tortilla sponsored by Gucci.

Luxury brands have a business model that's less about $20,000 purses than $50 perfumes. The $20,000 purses get the press and the brand value; $50 perfumes keep the whole machine running. That's why you have McQueen for Target, and a Louis Vuitton/Supreme collaboration. Anything that's luxe or conceptual can feel unwelcoming and pretentious, even beyond the price point, and turn people off. Luxe conceptual is the opposite of chicken and biscuits; it's the antithesis of a nice, familiar egg. That's why eggs will outlive us all.

I built my career off an egg. I sell comfort and nostalgia, and my restaurants are edible time capsules that take my customers back to my childhood—and maybe theirs. From there, I was able to be ambitious and creative, and play with ideas that attempted to reconceptualize the very nature of dining out. But everything was always anchored to that sense of comfort, safety, and familiarity. At the heart of eggs, chicken and biscuits, and spiked cereal milk is a grown ass man remembering what it was like to be worried at night when he was a kid. A kid who clung to comfort food as a way to feel better about his entire future, and still does.

HAPPY MEALS

By now, my Sarahpist and I had developed a pretty clear idea of what was going on with me, mentally.

"Anxiety disorder, not otherwise specified" was my core pervasive issue, with OCD as an additional storyline (awesome!), and let's not forget the occasional bouts of depression (more fun!).

We also learned that in relationships, I have something known as an "anxious attachment style." Sexy, right? It's not so much a disorder as it is how I relate to the people I'm romantically involved with. I was fascinated, learning just how many different ways my childhood programming had completely fucked up every aspect of my adult life, including my sex life. Because of shit that had happened literally twenty years ago, I was managing to irritate my girlfriends, and I felt incredibly stressed by relationships, even when I was trying hard to be a good boyfriend.

"So there's anxious, secure, and avoidant attachment types," Sarah told me, via Zoom. She'd just gotten a new tattoo on her butt—she posted it on her Instagram, that's how I knew. It read, "I SEE GOOD SPIRITS I SEE BAD SPIRITS." I loved her more with each session.

"You're anxiously attached, which means you are into intimacy on the surface, but you also feel very scared that people are going to abandon you, and when you're triggered you act out. You bail, or you spiral, or try to control outcomes."

"That sounds on brand," I said, wondering if anyone else I knew was this way.

"You're just easily triggered, and the avoidant types are too."

She explained how when you're anxiously attached, instead of enjoying relationships, you find yourself constantly on edge, worrying whether it will last, reading between the lines of every text, trying so hard to manage the relationship you forget to take care of yourself. You're always plotting grand romantic gestures as a way to manufacture the reassurance you need to make yourself feel at ease.

"So I do relationships the same way I do my business. The customer is always right."

"The deeper issue, Jeremy, is that you actually have a deep fear of intimacy even though you might behave as though it's the one thing you crave the most. It's linked to the neuroses that you developed as a result of childhood factors, and you just have to be mindful about that."

"Are there meds I should be taking?"

"No, we don't medicate attachment styles. But neuroplasticity is real. You can change your thoughts, Jeremy. You already are. You're adopting different ways of being. Softening the edges of those spirals you find yourself in. You're rewiring your brain."

"How important is it for people to be aware of their attachment styles?" I asked, fascinated. "Is this a core thing that we should all try to figure out about ourselves, or is it just some trendy thing that people talk about on the internet right now?"

"Actually, I think it's a core thing," she said. "And I'd really love to see an uptick in men's awareness about emotional avoidance. Attachment styles are not a diagnosis, though, and I really want to emphasize that there are gray territories. There are some people that are purely anxious and some people that are purely avoidant, right? But most of us are in a range from secure. If we got some relatively good love growing up, or we've done at least some work on ourselves, we're probably capable of some level of secure attachment, and often, we become more secure by being in a secure relationship. You're only as healthy as the relationship that you're in. If we gravitate toward really broken people, that's often a mirror of our own brokenness."

"Oh, shit. Really?"

"Often, but not always. We can all find ourselves in bad relationships because we don't recognize red flags. But we often feel them in our bodies, did you know that?"

"Wait—our body recognizes red flags even when our minds don't?"

"Yeah! You might go on a date with someone, and everything they did seemed fine and totally on the mark, but there's just this feeling, a red flag in your body that says, *warning*. You might have been picking up on body language, something on an animal level. Trusting those signs, trusting those feelings, is important. Like if something feels a little off, it's worth examining that, paying attention to it, and seeing what's going on."

All of a sudden, a thought popped into my head. A cheeseburger-shaped thought. This often happens when I feel flooded with information.

"Sarah, I'm feeling something in my body. I'm hungry."

"Oh," she said. "I forgot about you and the burgers."

"Sarah, it's all about the burgers. It always has been."

I spend a LOT of money at McDonald's. McDonald's is my emotional support multinational, and we all have one. A truly basic, mass-market pleasure. Are you a grown adult who eats Lucky Charms? When you got COVID-19, did you find yourself craving Annie's Mac & Cheese? Or, like me, in moments of existential chaos, does your mind immediately turn to Ronald McDonald? (No wonder so many of us are in therapy. We've been haunted by a creepy clown all our lives.)

My McDonald's cravings and the ritual of fulfilling those cravings are genuinely a through line in my life, embarrassing as that is when I see it written down. But damn. Those sweet, juicy slices of patty-shaped support, the bliss of optimized product delivery, supply chain and flavor experience, plus the knowledge that 2.3 billion people are eating this shit alongside me, every month—it's getting me worked up.

I'm going to go on the record and say that McDonald's is a spiritual experience for me. A community. A super greasy tranquilizer. I'm lovin' it. The shit worked, and it made me happy, every time. Now they're delivering? Game OVER. Sometimes I cheat—maybe it's part of being anxiously attached—but I do also hit In-N-Out on a fairly regular basis. In fact, there have been actual articles written about my In-N-Out order. Animal Style Double-Double, no lettuce, no tomato, add raw onion and extra cheese. I get my fries well-done and add on an ice water, because I like to be healthy. But guess what—I think I prefer Shake Shack to In-N-Out, and—

"Jeremy, are you still with me?" Sarah said and I came back to earth, my eyes still a little glazed over, my stomach rumbling . . .

"I want a Big Mac with extra cheese, two cheeseburgers, chicken nuggets, fries. I am literally on a diet today, Sarah, and that's what I'm going to get."

McDonald's is my chicken and biscuits. My comfort blanket. My Snuggie. And if I'm honest, it's what inspired Breakfast for Dinner. Remember when McDonald's stock went up a trillion percent after they announced they were doing breakfast all day long? That moment stayed with me. I remembered that joy (it was a real moment in my life), when I realized I could buy an Egg McMuffin at midnight, and that moment influenced one of my most important business decisions. Nighthawk was my own version of McDonald's Breakfast All Day, but elevated, a few steps above IHOP, with a full bar and old school hip hop on the jukebox. My anxious mind had made it easy for me to become addicted to the calming properties of a McDonald's meal, and my creative mind was funneling the whole feeling into a business plan that made a name for the adult me. If that's not some chicken and biscuits shit, I don't know what is.

Unless you're fully healed and had a perfect childhood, you're probably still just a kid on the inside, crying for your Happy Meals or your Frosties, yearning for the thing that will transport you back to a more innocent place. Statement jewelry will come and go, but a McDouble is forever. Gimme a cold soda, a hot burger, and salty fries—the eternal highs of salt, fat, and sugar—and show me God the holy trinity, father, son, and holy spirit, in a brown paper bag.

Remember when Travis Scott made a line of McDonald's merch? T-shirts with Cactus Jack in the Golden Arches? A $90 McNugget body pillow. A brown work jacket with "Billions and Billions Served" embroidered on the back, $128. And a Meal, $6, for a souped-up Quarter Pounder with Cheese, fries with barbecue sauce, and a Sprite. Did it make Travis Scott any less original and forward-thinking as an artist? Is he any less the hip hop artist who claims not to be a hip hop artist and cites Radiohead's Thom Yorke as a major influence? Or did doing some basic AF themed burger cross-marketing literally just earn him a shitload more money so he could carry on being his authentic self?

Haters will say that McDonald's is a multinational junk food cartel contributing to global obesity with products that give you greasy skin and a salt hangover. Which is true. But it's an empire that was built on kids' emotions. Kids who grow up and want to remember that same feeling. Simple, predictable, safe, and basic AF.

That chicken and biscuits shit, again.

VODKA SODA FOR PRESIDENT

When I launch a restaurant (or any business) I think of it like a record.

The kitchen is the recording studio.

The chefs are production.

Front of house staff are the backup singers and dancers.

And on the menu, instead of snacks, you got tracks.

You need an anthem, a commercial single that's going to get played in clubs. The one that's going to get stuck in people's heads, and get you on late-night talk shows and shit. That's your chicken and biscuits–inspired crowd-pleaser. The single that reminds people of other songs that they already like, but it's somehow different and better.

Then you have the Pastrami Agnolotti, the B-side that hardcore believers will be talking about in ten years on Discogs, but makes everyone else say, "Oh, look how creative! But I'll take the chicken and a vodka soda, thanks."

Personally, I don't drink anymore—unless I want to go to spiral town—but even though I'm a foodie, I'm not mad at simple cocktails like vodka soda, provided the ingredients are good. Mixology and the ascendence of the hyper-complicated cocktail never sat right with me, as you know. It always felt anti–chicken and biscuits. Snobby. Elitist. And not in a fun way. I still think mixology sucks. I don't want seventeen fucking ingredients in my cocktail. I like straight booze. I'll use sage and lavender in my moisturizer. I don't want my cocktail to have more ingredients than my Aesop shower gel. But for a long time, I felt like I was in the minority.

It was around 2010 when LA's restaurant scene really started to develop a cocktail-driven subculture, in which mixologists joined the ranks of chefs. The city became one of the top cocktail destinations in the country, and talented bartenders (like Jared) began flocking here from all over the US. These kids were known for reviving ancient recipes from the Gilded Age, studying cocktail guides from the 1890s (which is when bartenders were first called mixologists) and using them as the basis for some truly ambitious, brilliant recipes for twenty-first-century cocktails.

There was a bartender in New York, Dale DeGroff, aka King Cocktail, who really got the modern cocktail movement started in the 1980s when he was working at New York's Rainbow Room, using high-quality ingredients to reimagine classic cocktails. He was the one who resurrected the term "mixologist" because he wanted notoriety from the press. The mixologists who followed in his wake were true artists. They would have spit on a vodka soda because they are shamans, initiates to a sacred craft, and they absolutely will not serve you anything mixed with Red Bull, unless the Red Bull has been deconstructed and turned into a foam that's infused with incense. Or something.

The mixologists that populated the LA bar scene of the 2010s said, "Fuck your vodka Red Bull, but how about a mandarin blossom vodka, prosecco and strawberries macerated in Grand Marnier, custom-blended to your tastes, and did you notice the copy of a mixology bible (a 1913 edition of *Straub's Manual of Mixed Drinks* or Ensslin's sixty-three-page *Recipes for Mixed Drinks*) sticking out of my pocket?"

Watching these mixologists make an Old Fashioned was like witnessing a ritual, and I didn't like how it was starting to infuse the scene with a sense of something exclusionary and overcomplicated, when maybe all people wanted to do was have a night out and dance, without thirty ingredients sloshing around in their belly, pairing poorly with their Oxys?

That's why when I opened Genesis, I kept things simple. No mixology, just simple drinks and good times. Chicken and biscuits in a pop-up concept that bridged the gap between bar and nightclub, hidden inside a vintage attic in Hollywood. It was popular, sometimes too popular, like that night in January 2016, when there were so many people, it got scary. We had booked a surprise appearance by Juicy J, and I guess word spread that Genesis was the place to go for a really good time that night, no BS, no cover, affordable drinks. Unfortunately, we were not equipped to handle the crowds that night, and all that love soon turned to hate.

The line was all the way down Hollywood, where it intersects with Ivar. It was a public disturbance. There were helicopters and they closed the street down. The lines to get in were legitimately scary, and I had to be escorted into the venue by police so that I wouldn't get murdered by the people that had been in line for three hours. In the end, people started pushing in and trashed the venue. It was maybe the worst, most anxiety-inducing experience of my professional life, and it was around then that I started to reconsider my entire future in bars and clubs.

But when it was simple, it was beautiful. I was harnessing the power of broke, painting the walls at Genesis myself because I had no money. We did it with no permits, the whole thing was basically illegal. A guerrilla-style bar opening. But after that crazy night, I had a feeling

I wouldn't be able to do that stuff much longer. Besides, the city had a magnifying glass on me now.

I was twenty-three going on twenty-four, and I had opened two bars in a year, trying to keep things simple and realizing how hard that really is to pull off effectively. Looking around me I saw a lot of really cool kids, smart, brilliant mixologists and innovators who were depressed, broke, and drunk or on drugs, because they refused to "sell out" and just make a fucking vodka tonic. Toward the end of his life, Jared was showing up to interviews in sunglasses because he'd been up all night. He devoted his life to his craft, his art; he pushed the boundaries and made the unknown until his comfort zone, his chicken and biscuits, became an unhealthy place to be.

THE COMFORT ZONE

Most people don't want to be reeducated. Most people have been cultivating their behaviors for twenty or thirty years, or more, figuring out their likes, dislikes, vices, and coping systems, and never venturing too far from them. You can only reeducate a consumer to a certain extent, and if you manage to do it, it usually only happens once in a while. Most people aren't going to eat at my restaurants more than three times a week.

Me, my emotional coping mechanism is McDonald's, but my regular comfort zone when I'm just chilling is sushi. I mean, I love sushi. Period. It traces back to the simplicity that I crave. Sushi is, after all, usually just a few ingredients, executed perfectly. And as I got older, as much as I love insane food and thinking outside the box, I realized I wasn't going to do that three, four times a week. It's exhausting.

The same thinking applies to how we present ourselves in the world, as individuals and creators. Sure, be a complicated, complex, nuanced, tortured artist, but ultimately, you have to distill the essence of yourself into something that people can connect with, or you'll never make money. And if you're reading this book, I'm assuming that's something that you want to do.

I am complicated as fuck, a multilayered dude full of contradictions, but people call me the Food Guy, and that has opened doors for me for years. I don't love being the Food Guy, I don't love reductionism, and I avoid pigeonholing myself, but it took years for me to get to a place where I could communicate who I was to people in terms they could quickly understand. In a one- or two-sentence log line that summed me up, and my story.

A Jewish, mixed-race, acutely anxious LA creative blends food with other media in order to create experiential conversations around culture that span art, music, and mental health.

Now let's break it down.

1. WHO: Your Authentic DNA, Specifically Expressed

Jewish, mixed-race, acutely anxious LA creative. That's me, in a nutshell. It wasn't until I acknowledged and owned my mental health struggles as part of my brand that I could feel truly comfortable about how I was presenting myself to the world. I'm not suggesting or pressing anyone to publicly reveal anything they don't feel ready to talk about, but the more authentic you are in your presentation, and the more specific you are in the words you choose to describe yourself, the more you're giving your audience to connect with.

2. WHAT: Your Chicken and Biscuits

What do you bring to the table?

I "blend food with other media."

That is the whole entire, basic-bitch chicken and biscuits of what I do.

I'm not the first, or the last person on earth to do this. But by paper-clipping it with my WHO, my Jewish, mixed-race, acutely anxious LA creativity, I'm creating something new, and authentically me.

3. WHY: Your Pasta Agnolotti

I do what I do for one reason: to create experiential conversations that span art, music, and, now, mental health.

This is your raison d'être. This is why you do what you do. This is the stuff that makes your heart beat faster—your true creative DNA combined with an action to create income and fulfillment.

This is the part where you get to feel like you're doing something different, making your mark, expressing yourself as an individual human being with a finite time on this planet, and the ability to make change, however large or small. It can be as simple as a sandwich, but it's *your* sandwich, it's *your* recipe, and there will never be anything more satisfying than watching someone put that thing in their mouth and smile.

7

FROM SCRAMBLED EGGS TO CAVIAR

Connecting the Dots Throughout Your Story

M Y RELATIONSHIP WITH EGGS GOES WAY BACK.

As a sperm, I had a very strong attraction to eggs—and that was just the beginning; I've been obsessed ever since.

I relate to eggs; like me, they're hearty, full of possibilities, hard on the outside, gooey on the inside.

Eggs have been the perfect muse as I've built my business story, a story that's inspired by the quest to create context, and spark conversations. Eggs provide me with a blank canvas upon which to unleash my imagination because there are a million and one ways to make them, break them, and tell a story.

Eggs, the kind laid by chickens, are ubiquitous, accessible, down to earth, and the way I create conversations around the humble chicken egg is to pull it out of the breakfast zone, and insert it into a fine dining environment, with added cocktails. Plus, they have a great profit margin—around 80 percent for a scramble.

Eggs, the kind laid by fish, aka caviar, are already luxe, evoking thoughts of money, cocaine, and oligarchs on yachts. Best paired with a bottle of Dom Pérignon, they're very thought-provoking for someone like me, who grew up with zero financial security. So the way I handle caviar is to paper-clip it with things that are lowbrow, commonplace, and proletarian. Items on my menus have included caviar pizza, caviar grilled cheese sandwiches, and in one episode of my online cooking show, *Beats for Breakfast,* I made a $2,000 Caviar Bagel using gold leaf, two types of premium caviar, and shaved fresh black truffle. Context is everything.

This might sound like a strange comparison, but eggs remind me of Jesus in terms of a product that's been branded and interpreted to death. I may be Jewish, but mad props to JC for building one of the most adaptable brands of all time. (By the way we didn't kill him, the Romans did. Just a reminder.) Jesus, like eggs, represents something ineffable. A thing that we haven't been able to completely define. Dude's a blank slate, crying out for interpretation. Is he a white guy with blue eyes who looks like he's in Pink Floyd and has a pet dinosaur? Is he Black and beautiful? His face is not fully definable, and therefore it's open to multiple forms of interpretation that have literally divided the world, but also brought people together.

Jesus is a projection of every individual who believes in him, and that is the genius of He Who Is Born Again On The Third Day, and eggs. We humans are just vacuums with gaps to be filled, and both have figured out how to satiate the hunger in our hearts and in our stomachs. Bitcoin, too, has a very religious feel to it. No one knows who created it. Most people still don't understand it, and it has a mysticism around it—my point is this: whether we're talking about the Bible or Bitcoin or scrambled eggs, it's all about the story. The meanings we assign to the things around us. The things we choose to do create moments along a narrative thread, and these moments tell the story of our lives. And whether it's a comedy, a tragedy, an indie, or a blockbuster, all depends on the shape of the dots that we're connecting, while building a story that lasts a lifetime.

Some Biblical shit.

ALL I SEE IS DOTS

Connecting the dots is part of my blueprint for evolution, both personal and professional. It's about searching for the main theme of your story, as you go along. And once you figure out what that is, you can use that information to plan your next step. When you're connecting dots, you're picking the smartest, smoothest way to elevate yourself from plain old scrambled eggs to your own personal beluga caviar. From carpenter's kid to Son of God. You're taking your core idea from dream, to execution, to maximum potential, and what's key is to do it in a way that makes sense.

When I was making experimental sauces in my mother's kitchen aged eleven, that was a dot along my timeline, even though I didn't know it then.

When I sat in my Prius in The Grove parking lot aged twenty-two, and realized I wanted to quit nightlife and go full force into food, that was another big ass dot.

When I was having a panic attack in the parking lot at Sugarfish, and realized it was time to seek help managing my anxiety disorder, that was another very important dot.

The morning I woke up, frustrated AF with the way some people perceived me—"I'm not a fucking trust fund kid!"—and decided I wanted to write a book about it, that was a dot. (Of course, it was completely my fault that people perceived me as a privileged rich kid, because that was an identity I'd cultivated as a way to mask the fact that I had, in fact, grown up broke. Karma's a bitch, and inauthenticity will always catch up to you.)

Connecting the dots is different from paper clip mentality.

Spiked Cereal Milk was born out of a paper clip mentality, but Spiked Cereal Milk ending up as a bottled mass-market product through content marketing—that's connecting the dots, and each dot contains its own little storyline.

The reason Spiked Cereal Milk worked was that it was selling people a time machine into their childhood. Like Jesus, my milky cocktail was filling the void and getting people high on life. Maybe you moved far away from home and Lucky Charms in milky rum reminded you of those special moments with your siblings at home, growing up and watching Saturday morning cartoons. That is what we were selling. The product, in my opinion, was somewhat overrated compared to the storytelling, which was perfect, if I do say so myself.

Spiked Cereal Milk as a bottled mass-market consumer product is in my fridge, right now, a prototype. The core idea taken to its maximum potential. The milk and alcohol are separated, but then you twist the bottom and shake it and it mixes. I'm trademarking it as a brand, then I'll license it out to a cocktail company, and then we'll do ice cream.

We only use oat milk now, of course—when we first started it used to be made with cow's milk. I'm lactose intolerant (Jews often have stomach issues) and I would be stunned, watching people pound three of those things, thinking, *how are you not shitting your brains out?* Anyway, bottling Spiked Cereal Milk is a dot connected to a theme that's been unfolding throughout the business story I've been developing all these years.

Thematic continuity is essential, you see.

Think about it: if I'd gone from Spiked Cereal Milk to, say, building robotic cats (yep, someone did that), that would not be connecting dots. Those would be unrelated dots, and they would confuse the theme. Your theme should be the thing that links your current idea to your prior one, while offering a pathway to the next. Because the overarching theme of my story is food, robotic cats would only make sense in my story if they were trained to deliver you eggs. Although I hope they figure that out one day, because that would be awesome.

DOTS UNDER PRESSURE

Decision-making is a constant process in modern life that takes place from when we wake up until we *decide* to go to bed. But when we're anxious, it becomes harder to see the wood for the trees, and have any perspective on what we're doing, let alone connect the dots that make up our story.

When we're anxious, we often make poor decisions or no decision at all, because intuition can be impaired in a state of anxiety. Anxiety may direct behavior toward the safest option, and guide you toward a dot that is a sideways step, rather than forward motion. Sometimes moving cautiously is the best way to go, but sometimes it's not, and that's when anxiety can stand in the way of you living your best life, because it's literally pulling you away from your dreams.

When we're anxious, we've fired up a set of structures in our brain called the limbic system, an area responsible for emotional responses, memory, and motivation. Your brain waves—delta, beta, theta, and gamma—flow in a measured rhythm during a positive stress state, but fall into "neurochemical chaos" during a negative stress state. Essentially, anxiety causes all function in your prefrontal cortex—the area of the brain responsible for influencing attention, impulsivity, memory, and more—to go haywire. And that's where our best reasoning, decision-making, and perspective come from.

When an anxious brain is in fight-or-flight mode, its overheated limbic system can cycle through an endless series of scary possibilities that affect decision-making. Scientists call that "amygdala hijack"—the amygdala is a part of the limbic system—and it's as though your prefrontal cortex has lost control of the vehicle altogether. When you're on amygdala hijack, you're spinning, paralyzed, unable to perceive reality with objective eyes. That's when we make emotionally driven decisions, which might not be our best decisions at all. The way to hack this response, apparently, is to cool off your brain before making decisions, giving your rational prefrontal cortex a chance to take control.

Easier said than done when you're trying to manage your business narrative while obsessing over the stray dog that just licked your shoe, which means you'll have to cancel a meeting to go get a rabies shot.

HANGRY FOR SUCCESS

People often ask me, "what do you do for a living?" and for a long time it was difficult for me to answer that question in a way that people understood, because since leaving nightlife, I've done so many different things.

Restaurants.

Podcasts.

TV.

NFTs.

Music.

What connects them all is food, and I ask new questions about food with every venture.

How does food transform our view of the world? How does food interact with all the other things I'm passionate about, from music to fashion, film, art, and tech?

I just launched a VR restaurant that you can walk around in and listen to my podcast while ordering chicken and biscuits. Someone else might file this concept under "weird tech." But because it's exploring food from a fresh angle, it totally fits with my hangry, food-obsessed narrative.

Another tech-ish concept: I'm working on an NFT collection that incorporates AI, enabling users to create sketch representations of different foods and build a virtual dinner party experience. You can create fictional characters that are cooking the meal, eating the meal, talking about the meal through audio, and it will allow people to feel like they're connecting through food. Even though there's nothing edible about the experience, it still makes sense as part of my story. It fits, and it feels authentic to Jeremy Fall™.

Fact: I have over a million followers, and 99.9 percent of them have never tried my food. If you read my DMs, you'll see that people are more interested in my playlist on Spotify, where I buy my clothes, and my journey with mental health than they are about my Cacio e Pepe.

My style, my playlist, and my anxiety didn't make my career, though, nor did they get me a book deal—my career in food did.

Food reverberates at the heart of every dot along my narrative timeline. And rather than being a limitation, this thematic specificity has allowed me to safely explore *beyond* food in my business, while still adhering to a storyline that makes sense to my investors as "on brand."

I hate the term "on brand," by the way. It represents a limiting mindset, in my opinion. If you're connecting the dots the right way, anything and everything can be "on brand," so long as it's an expression of the core theme in your story. Like what Veuve Clicquot has done with champagne—the brand found a way to sell luxury champagne for fifty dollars, a bottled attainable luxury, and mainstreamed champagne to the degree that even people who don't know about champagne will say, "I want a bottle of Veuve." That's my kind of branding flex. My kind of story.

THE "WHY"

People care much more about WHY you do something than WHAT you're doing.

Take Apple, for instance. Apple is all about "think different," the advertising slogan the company used from 1997 to 2002, which is still printed on the back of iMac boxes. Notice how the people at Apple aren't talking about *what* they're selling; they're talking about their story, the creed that Steve Jobs preached. Think different is the why not the what, and that's a big part of what people are buying when they put down a grand for an iPhone. It's because they want to inhabit a context that feels boundary-pushing because Steve Jobs established himself as a mysterious demigod in an Issey Miyake turtleneck and glasses that had a vision for completely changing the world. People wondered, "How did he do this? He didn't tell me exactly what to do, but he made me feel something that made me think differently, and want to do something different and create my own path." Apple made a $1,000 phone mainstream. How the fuck did they do that, without presenting themselves as luxury? They have beautiful stores and sleek design; Apple feels elevated and high-end, but it doesn't feel like you're walking into Cartier or Gucci, because the story is different.

Anyone can make a T-shirt, right? But there's a reason the Supreme logo means more than most other T-shirt logos. It's the context the brand built around it. The WHY. The Supreme story is built around the street kids and skate culture, which attracts people who want to connect to that story, even if they've never skateboarded in their life. People buy into the symbolism behind that red logo and what it represents to them, because the company always told its story in the right way, with authenticity, and never veered off course, thematically. That is how that little red symbol became known around the world.

Yes, I cried when Mufasa died, but when it comes to successful storytelling, Disney obviously springs to mind, and I don't even mean the actual movies. People forget that Disney didn't invent most of the stories that made it big. The Brothers Grimm, nineteenth-century German writers Jacob and Wilhelm, came up with a lot of them. Cinderella, Rapunzel, Snow White, Sleeping Beauty, Little Red Riding Hood—all of them with the classic formula. Good wins over evil, innocence kicks oppression's ass. Disney didn't come up with the formula, but it perfected it and made "feel-good" and "happy endings" its WHY. Its social narrative.

Today, it might seem as though Disney is all over the place as a company. It's Mickey Mouse and Aladdin and Star Wars and ESPN and National Geographic and theme parks and cruise ships and Hulu and the Muppets. But somehow, it's all very Disney, because they are slick storytellers, above all, and that's the theme of Disney's own success story.

People love Tesla for many reasons too, but usually because they have some interest in the story of Elon Musk. The character he has become in the media. Yes, it's a car, but it's also a story. A series of dots that started with Musk's daddy issues and led to him marrying Grimes and becoming the wealthiest man on earth. As a tormented genius who is part superhero, part total nerd, Musk's story resonates with many people, especially the underdogs who want to be cool and get the alt-girl of their dreams.

If your happily ever after, from a career perspective, is about making money and healing your mind and shifting the culture, then it's going to help you get there faster if the dots in your story are painted in a palette of colors that look and feel good together. Sometimes literally. If you chose the color green for your brand, for instance, ask yourself why *this* emerald green? Should it be palm tree green, because you're from California and you're inspired by the beach and the boulevards? That's what I'm talking about. That level of specificity should feed into every dot of your business identity. Even if it's very subtle.

That being said, curated tone, voice, graphics, color palettes—all the traditional external branding elements—do not supersede authenticity. Over-curation goes against authenticity, and when something is over-planned, it can appear contrived. Great stories come from the heart. Being spur-of-the-moment, filterless, and "felt cute might delete later" pushes the "this is me" storyline that should be at the core of what you do.

And as you're defining your place in the grand scheme of things, do the work of a Hollywood storyteller on your business. Analyze the twists and turns of your story, and the mechanics of who your lead characters really are. Once you see that and make sense of it, you'll have an entire blueprint for your future, and a way to understand your past.

DOTS INTO DIAMONDS

Let's go back to that dot from the year of our Lord 2016, when I was twenty-two, sitting in my car in the parking lot at The Grove, mad as hell with my career in nightlife. I was done with drunk people throwing up on my shoes. I hated that some people thought I was a poser. I'd become a pro at skewing people's perception of me, and manipulating reality, hiring paparazzi to get into the Grammys, writing a "success" story that I no longer wanted to be a part of. And I was drinking too much booze—I don't anymore, at all. No coffee, no drugs, either. I mainly drink matcha americanos with rose water—it's good for the skin.

"I don't know what to do with my life," I thought, sitting in my Prius. "I don't know what my 'thing' is anymore."

I had done a great job of turning bullshit into an art form, but my bullshit was inauthentic bullshit, and I was surrounded by inauthentic bullshitters because birds of a feather flock together. Did I really want that to be the theme of my life? People were calling me a douchebag, a hipster, but I'm not a fucking hipster, holier than thou, trying to pretend they're broke because being rich isn't "cool." Six-figure hipsters is what I call them, you know—starving artist trust funders who call themselves indie and talk about the struggle but also use natural deodorant that's nineteen dollars; people from Brentwood pretending they're from Inglewood, appropriating culture, oozing inauthenticity, and somehow I was surrounded by them. Playing a part, laughing along, wearing dumb leather gloves to be "cool" when I didn't actually like leather gloves.

"Who is Jeremy Fall, what does he do, what does he like?" I asked myself. "Where do I belong?"

I thought about it, realizing I was many things, and it was in my power to decide which identity I wanted to focus on. Which story I wanted to tell. I wrote a free-form list, trying to figure out who the fuck I was, and it read a little like this:

I paint my nails.

I'm straight.

I'm a germophobe.

I'm always in control, but I often feel out of control.

I own the room, but I'm always wondering if people like me.

I have this weird cough.

My best friend says I can sell a paper bag as a Birkin.

I'm good at creating things that people feel like they want, things that feel attainable but elevated.

I love the underground.

Amanda Lepore performed at my bar and that still makes me happy.

I'm drinking too fucking much.

I hate that the price of limes has gone up and no one is putting them in margaritas.

I was getting nowhere. So I tried something different. I asked myself this:

If I had a billion dollars, what would I spend my money on? This time, my answers told me everything I needed to know.

Food.

Room service.

Restaurants.

Dinner parties at my house.

My dreams were all centered on food.

"I am going to become a Food Guy! I am going to change the way people eat and receive food. I am going to break the walls down. I am going to be the guy who does food, but who also designs shoes, and does stuff in tech. Like Pharrell, but in the restaurant space."

The more I thought about it, the more excited I became. I'd always loved the context around food. Bringing people together. Having people over, whether I was ordering Domino's pizza or flying in a wagyu steak from Japan. My dinner parties always started at 2 p.m. and went on until 11 p.m. because food was my forever passion. Feeding people brought me more joy than anything else. I started to think about layering, not just flavors—salt, fat, acid, heat—but ideas within food. Affordable shit that sounds fancy. A burger but instead of ketchup, you combine liquid smoke and ketchup, then we cook the patty in brown butter, and we serve cheese on the side, like an American cheese fondue with black garlic, and there has to be a way to pair sriracha peanut butter. Layering, layering, layering, a whole mess of paper clips flooded my mind as I realized:

I'd found the next dot! This was the authentic ME! Awesome!

Now, how the fuck was I going to make it part of my story, which had nothing to do with food? Because I had no experience other than working at my mom's café, I HAD to connect the dots somehow in order to convince people to get on board. So I injected nightlife energy into my vision for how food could be—meaning, curated music, a buzzy atmosphere, late hours—and suddenly, it made sense to everyone. The dots were connected, and that's when investors started to come on board and support my completely insane vision to open a restaurant. Because the dots between this new chapter of my story, and the last, were connected.

I was thrilled, even though it meant leaving behind the life and relationship I'd created with Jared, who was becoming angrier and more depressed, just like I had been. Not long after he and I parted ways, he moved to Reno, and we would text or chat on the phone here and there. In one of our last conversations, I said, "Bro, there's always a place for you in whatever we do, you were the first person to believe in me." But I knew he and I were on different paths, even though I wasn't sure where either of us was ultimately headed.

I heard stories here and there. That he put cameras all around his house and was doing a lot of DMT—hey, that shit works for a lot of people, but it didn't seem to be doing him any favors. I felt some guilt around it all. Here I was, moving in this new direction, connecting dots that seemed to be leading me to a happier place. But it seemed like Jared had found himself stuck in a dot that was rapidly turning into a black hole, consuming him. I've come up with a million theories as to why Jared's mental state took him to the place of no return. But no one except him will ever know the truth about what was going on in his head, the day he decided to leave this earth. So I'll just leave it right there.

THIS SHIT IS A MOVIE

Hey, did you ever see *Fall Story*? It's like *Toy Story*, but more foody, and it stars the Food Guy (me) as he bounces along the dots in his universe.

Food Guy loves extravagant meals, many of which are either caviar or McDonald's, and Easter is his favorite holiday, because eggs (also, Jesus was a Jew).

Food Guy is super creative and has big goals, something his friend, Miss Paper Clip, loves to help him out with.

Rounding out the cast is Mr. Loose Balloon, brilliant but spacey and always floating away into the stratosphere.

Bob, my imposter syndrome, appears throughout, and he's always telling me I don't belong, which makes me act like an arrogant asshole in social situations because I'm making up for the fact that I don't think I belong. Thanks, Bob!

And every good story needs its villain, so here comes Alan. My anxiety, personified.

Alan was the antagonist and for a long while, he was definitely winning. Food Guy was just doing his thing, trying to get from dot to dot, then Alan came along like a category 5 hurricane. Soon he was steering the ship, running the show, turning up to dinner uninvited, coughing everywhere, having meltdowns, and driving too fast.

"Everything's happening, happening, happening!" he'd yell in my ear, and it was intoxicating. I felt like Winona Ryder in *Girl, Interrupted*, and Alan was my Angelina Jolie character, a diagnosed sociopath known for her cruel manipulation and psychological abuse. Other days, Alan felt like Ferris Bueller and I was his depressed best friend, Cameron, being forced to have fun.

Alan made me believe I always had to be busy, having ideas, planning ways to treat my friends, obsessing over which book to read or which show to watch. Alan is why I love Christmas so much, because it's stressful and hectic as fuck, and you get to give a ton of presents.

Alan made me feel like my life was exciting, because there were never two days that were remotely similar.

"This feels right, Alan!" I'd say.

And he'd say, "DO IT! CARPE DIEM!" in our R-rated movie (warnings: mental illness, self-harm).

As much as my Sarahpist says my childhood affected my mental makeup, I actually think Alan has been around from the day I was born. My mom told me that when I was a toddler, if I wanted more food, I would start pulling my hair out. I was three and the biggest shithead, hangry as hell, and awkward around everyone. Kids would play on the playground and I didn't want to join in because I felt weird and just wanted to be around my mom. The first time I ever slept over at a friend's house I was six or seven years old, and I had a full-on panic attack and had to go home. I think it was baby Alan, playing games with my head, even then.

Alan never gave me time to think, and before long the bond between us felt unbreakable. Alan never had any interest in changing, even as he started to wear me out. Even as life became unbearable, even as he began to ruin my relationships and cloud my decision-making. Alan kept framing our life together as an adventure—to infinity and beyond!—but soon I started to realize he wasn't the friend I thought he was.

When I got into therapy, that's when the plot shifted. Obviously, Alan was pissed about how much time I was spending with my Sarahpist because she was helping me get clear on what my story actually looked like. My dots were all over the place, and the lines between them were jagged and chaotic—products of an anxious mind battling to escape a toxic alliance. Still, though, it was hard for me to hate Alan. I made excuses for him, even wondered if my ego was the issue, not my anxiety.

I told Sarah I thought I was a narcissist, but she shot that down pretty fast.

"Narcissists usually don't think they're narcissists," she said.

"There's always exceptions to every rule. I must be a self-aware narcissist."

"Let me ask you this—what if someone forgot about your birthday, would you throw a temper tantrum, or have a conversation with them?"

"Neither. I'd probably buy them a gift to make myself feel better."

"Jeremy, I don't think you're a narcissist."

"But I think I'm the best! And the worst!"

"That's just your ego, combined with imposter syndrome. Look, my priority is to help your thoughts slow down. You don't have to keep running. You don't have to feel like everything's going to collapse tomorrow."

"IT *IS* GOING TO COLLAPSE TOMORROW!" Alan screamed in my head.

"Don't worry, Jeremy, we're going to understand your anxiety, and find a way to reposition it so it's not governing your life."

Obviously, we're still writing the movie, and Food Guy still has anxiety; he will *always* have some anxiety. My whole life is a brainstorm. I am constantly exercising that muscle that makes me think, and rethink bigger, every time. And I still wash my hands a lot because of my OCD. I still see all possible scenarios ahead of me, all the ways I can fall, but I know I'm falling upwards, and none of this creates panic in me, nor does it affect my decision-making and thought processes like it did when Alan was in charge.

I can plan ahead more and look backwards with fresh, analytical eyes. When I experience doubt, it doesn't frighten me. Doubting yourself, and rethinking what you know, can be a good thing sometimes, because every great idea has the possibility of being improved. There's always going to be an element of carpe diem in business, of just seeing and seizing the opportunities that are in front of you. There's beauty in letting your story write itself instead of always wanting to write the next chapter. There's magic when you let each chapter unfold, versus trying to write the last page of your story. But not when Alan is in charge.

And I've found that when I no longer stress about what feel like missed opportunities, or closed chapters, things often come back around. Connecting dots often travel in circular patterns, a spiral staircase, snakes and ladders. You'll sometimes go up and down, and find yourself echoing aspects of yourself, reimagining moments from long ago and repurposing them for your now.

It all fits with my slogan—everyday, redesigned. I can make you care about a kitchen towel or a water bottle or an egg. A thing you didn't care about before. I can reposition your thinking, and I did the same with my anxiety. Because I'm no longer being ruled by Alan, it's made me bold enough to follow my story, no matter what other storylines are beckoning. I prefer the way I am pursuing my narrative now that I'm in control of my anxiety, instead of the other way around.

But the anxiety has its own dot, and always will. I can't connect the dots of my life and build this through line based on an authentic version of myself without acknowledging my mental illness and how it has affected my journey. If I connect those dots, it's easy to see that Alan pushed me towards facing myself. Alan allowed this to become a bigger Disney story, one where there's a happy ending.

In case you were wondering, Alan's in rehab, living his best life. He still pops up, screaming in my ear.

"DON'T FORGET TO WASH YOUR HANDS OR YOU'RE GOING TO GET IMPETIGO AGAIN LIKE YOU DID WHEN YOU WERE A LITTLE KID!"

But he's just turned down the volume. I like to think he's doing some mindfulness meditation. Maybe a little psilocybin therapy. Whatever it takes.

8

STEAK, BACON, AND BLACK NAIL POLISH

Toxic Masculinity and the Neurodivergent Man

MANLY AS FUCK MELTDOWN

Professional kitchens, as we know, have always been pressure cookers: hot, sweaty, stressful. The caricature of a head chef is angry, full of piss and vinegar, unable to control his temper. He shouts at his staff for the most minor of reasons, and anger has made media icons out of screaming, intimidating, unhinged fuckholes. These guys who literally throw knives in the kitchen and blame the pressure cooker environment. But is it necessary to traumatize the people around you in the name of a perfect carbonara? Why is there this acceptance that "oh, you're in a kitchen—if you can't stand the heat, get out." Does it really need to be like that?

Gordon Ramsay's rants are often excused as merely an expression of his alpha male perfectionism. There's a sense of "this is how it is; we're just going to make this an unworkable environment, and if you can't handle it, that's your problem." People rise up through the ranks and become abusers and gatekeepers themselves. "Well, I had to pay my dues . . . and so will you." But just because you went through something, and maybe had to take a beating to get to where you are today, doesn't mean that you should enforce those appalling standards on others. We're all on our own path, and you can actually create change within your industry by being more supportive of young people coming into it, and not subjecting them to any of the bad practices you had to deal with. Break the paradigm.

To anyone outside of the restaurant bubble, that culture can appear somewhat deranged. Those aren't just sharp words, that's actual abuse. Unfortunately, the problem with kitchens is cultural. In a restaurant, abuse isn't just tolerated; it is aspirational. And it's been part of the system from the very start.

French Chef Auguste Escoffier introduced the "brigade system" of kitchen hierarchy in the late nineteenth century, and literally modeled it after an army. This brought a sense of discipline, law, and order to kitchens, but also concentrated power in the hands of assholes, who were untrained for leadership. By the way, the kitchen isn't supposed to be a war zone, dudes. It's just lunch.

In the 1990s, Marco Pierre White, the youngest chef to have been awarded three Michelin stars, became the poster child for assholes who cook. He described his kitchen as his "theatre of cruelty" and he shouted, swore, threw food and glass bottles, and slashed chefs' whites with knives. Chefs were literally hung on hooks by their aprons or thrown in dumpsters. "Discipline is born out of fear" was his motto.

His protégé was Gordon Ramsay, who he made cry once—and there began the cycle of abuse. Ramsay also made a career out of screaming at people until they, too, cried.

Anthony Bourdain, though, he was different. He possessed that supreme confidence that is the key through line of what society deems to be masculine. But he never needed to scream about it. The motorcycles, the tatted sleeves, hanging with rock stars and presidents— Bourdain was just super cool. Super manly. My kind of American idol, much more so than the maniacal chefs throwing shit in the kitchen.

In 2000, Bourdain's *Kitchen Confidential* detailed the toxic world of New York restaurants, and became a bible for bad-boy chefs. But Bourdain himself wrote that it "was not a story about a particularly good or commendable career. . . . It validates a lot of bad behavior." The self-reflection was beginning, sort of. Was bullying, domineering behavior justified, or even necessary, people whispered? The term "toxic masculinity" wasn't much of a thing back then. Few people were aware of how these cultures, whether they're in kitchens, boardrooms, or writers' rooms, fully traumatized everyone involved. It took the food business a long ass time to realize that people actually perform better when they're happy, rather than terrified. How many potential future stars of the industry quit after being bullied out of the system? How many women walked away thanks to men who had been taught that unhealthy work environments were normal?

But what does it mean to be a man like Bourdain? One who is extraordinarily articulate and perceptive and badass, but who still has very little space in which to address his emotional vulnerability? Being emo didn't fit the Bourdain brand. It wasn't what the people wanted. In these cases, where a man is both strong and sensitive, being celebrated for your masculinity can result in a worst-case scenario. In Bourdain's case, he drank to excess despite being a recovered heroin addict, and in June 2018, he died by suicide.

Being an alpha male hero puts you in a position where you're supposed to be tough and silent, all the time. It means you're not always fully equipped to deal with feelings, especially when your cool, badass image might be compromised by any admission of vulnerability. That's what makes tragedies. That's what makes men victims of their own perfect masculinity.

Working in the food industry, I tried to push past the stereotypes. I stayed cool, mostly. My staff was happy. I wanted working for me to feel like fun. It's strange, being a mix of typical dude and sensitive, all at once. For years, the only way to handle it was to keep the two sides separate. I rode my anxiety roller-coaster behind closed doors. No one except my doctor and my girlfriend knew that my cough was an anxiety cough. When my thoughts spiraled in the shower, that was just between me and my Aesop body wash. And when I drove like a maniac, I could pretend I was in the flow, finding creative ways to get through traffic, seeing what my engine could do.

But I'm ashamed to say, there were a few instances when my untreated anxiety and inherent toxic masculinity did bubble over and make themselves very apparent to the people around me. Of course, as a man in the food business, I had permission to express it in one very specific way. Rage.

I had opened a restaurant called Easy's at the Beverly Center, thanks to $3.5 million of investment funding. The vision was cool, a mix of vintage Americana style and West Coast culture to create a new kind of diner, with simple but elevated twists on classic comfort food, referencing icons from Tupac to the Fonz.

One day, my investor team flew in from Michigan to have dinner at Easy's and check out what I'd created. Obviously, it was a crucially important evening, and I needed to make sure everything ran as smoothly as possible. Before they arrived, I briefed the servers and kitchen staff on what was happening, and made sure everyone was on board. Tonight was our night to shine!

The investors arrived, sat down, and ordered their cocktails, which they loved. Then they picked a bunch of stuff from the menu to try. Twenty minutes went by, and no food had come out, so they called the server over.

"Hey, just wondering how long before . . ."

"Your food will be out shortly, my apologies!" she said.

The server came up to me and said the kitchen was being slow, so I went back there and asked the chefs to speed things up.

A little later, I got a text from one of the investors at the table.

"Jeremy, we're starving! What's going on?"

I had specifically told my staff to take care of this table as though their lives depended on it. What the fuck was happening?

I headed to the kitchen and, on my way, found the server in tears.

"They were mean to me! They were calling me names!"

"Who?"

"The guys in the kitchen! They got mad because I told them they needed to hurry up!"

I marched into the kitchen where the ticket for my investors' table was sitting there. My chefs were literally taking selfies of each other's butts.

"WHAT THE FUCK ARE YOU DOING! HOW DARE YOU MAKE MY SERVER CRY!"

They turned around, surprised to hear me scream. I never, ever raise my voice to my staff, but on this occasion, I'm pretty sure the entire restaurant could hear.

Then, it was like an out-of-body experience as I found myself picking up and throwing anything I could get my hands on. Cast-iron pans. A colander. Anything. It was surreal for everyone, including me. After a few moments, I stopped and came back to earth. Then I walked out and told the investors their food would be right out. And yes, their meals did come out incredibly fast after that.

Immediately afterwards, I asked my business partner to call HR and our attorney to tell them what I'd done. This was a serious incident, and I had behaved atrociously. None of the employees filed a report, and no one quit. In fact, when interviewed by HR, they all took my side, including the chefs who I had freaked out at. They knew I'd treated them well in the past, and they knew they had let me down on an important night. I was infinitely grateful we could all learn and put it behind us but still—there was no fucking excuse for my behavior (although, granted, they were being irresponsible and unprofessional and not doing their jobs). It was a sobering, frightening moment for me, realizing I could lose control like that. Like one of the toxic chef bro, "typical dude" douchebags I had told myself I would never be.

JUST THE TYP DUDE

Typical dudes like money, the way gasoline smells, and the way tires taste. Beer is big, although I personally don't drink anymore—if I have one drink, the next day my mental health will totally regress and I might act out and spend money on bracelets that don't fit, and then

I'll be depressed about it. So drinking is a no-no. Mainly, though, typical dudes do not share their feelings. That's perhaps the defining characteristic. Typical dudes are only allowed—by society and themselves—to be angry or neutral, and any kind of panic attack or vulnerable emotion must be kept secret, because it will be perceived as weak and unmanly.

Mainstream society, as we know, is fundamentally homophobic and misogynistic. It affiliates gayness and femininity with a lack of strength, even though the opposite is true, because to be gay in a homophobic world is to be tough as fuck, and to be a woman in an anti-woman world is also to be tough as fuck. But to be a typical dude in a world that is constantly grooming you for material success, alpha status, and power—that's just fool's gold. There's very little room for feelings in the mainstream masculinity paradigm, which is a big part of the reason I have anxiety disorder and am on medication.

But it's okay—just keep making that money, dudes, because that's all that matters. The awards. The houses. The boats. The shoes. Yes, modern dudes might say they support equality and present themselves as evolved bros, but all too often it's a surface, performative kind of evolution that doesn't address the core issue. Which is that underneath all that ego-driven posturing, we fucking hate ourselves, because we'll never be good enough.

The toxicity of it all really became clear to me when I was working in bars and nightlife. Some nights, I'd come home and ask myself, *are club promoters basically just glorified pimps?* I mean, it's such a weird setup: "Girls, come on in, and you'll get free drinks from the rich guy, who wants the girls, and pays the club a huge amount of money to bar owners who brokered the thing."

In Hollywood bottle service, there were guys we called "buyers," usually an older successful actor, someone very wealthy. A lot of them don't even drink, although they like to spray champagne and show off. It's a peacock move; it's flexing your wealth. A promoter might connect me to Johnny Buyer, because I owned a bar or ran the door.

"Yo, Johnny's in town and he wants to spend, what can we do?"

"Sure, I'll set him up."

Johnny would come in and spend $50k, and a ton of pretty girls would sit at Johnny's table, and flirt, which would make Johnny feel like a boss. The women were usually very proactive, because they, like all of us, were suckers for fame, money, and free booze.

There's a guy in Hollywood who is a famous actor's personal promoter. His entire job is to book tables for this actor, and every time he does, the bar owner has to pay him $10,000 cash, because you know this actor is going to spend at least $50,000. Meanwhile, we would pay the promoter out in cash, 20 percent of the actor's spend and then I'd pay my cocktail waitresses, who were making around $3,000 a night, although I've seen some of those girls walk away with $5,000 a night. I was glad they were making a good living, and if anyone ever groped my staff, *ever*, they would be 86ed.

Still, it made me uncomfortable. If a guy came into the club and was spending $100,000 and wanted blow, then you had to introduce him to the blow guy. If he wanted to go home with someone, you'd have to introduce him to the girls who would. I knew there were clubs in Hollywood with little rooms upstairs where men would bring girls up from the club and have sex with them on "fuck pads," and some of these girls were young. It was sleazy as fuck, and that's why I avoided participating in the bottle service system as much as I possibly could.

That's why I wanted to open bars that were different. That's why I never, ever, hit on my staff or anything like that. But it was impossible to completely avoid the feeling that I was part of a dirty world, and the only way I could escape was to completely leave that world behind.

Of course, I know I have a long way to go. I came of age in industries that, for the most part, completely refused to address toxic masculinity. As a man, I'm still very much a part of the paradigm—I'm driven by ego, and I still long for money and success, because that's my conditioning. For years, I publicly embodied swagger as often as I could. I lied, to myself and the world around me. I acted like I was cool, I was confident, like I didn't give a shit. I did everything I thought necessary for me to be recognized as a "Real G." And that meant conforming to over-the-top, alpha male culture. That meant keeping my mouth shut, even when things didn't feel right. It was primal and animalistic, my need to win. I became addicted to a toxic mindset, and then I put it in a kitchen, and turned up the heat.

KITCHEN NIGHTMARES

I was at Nighthawk one night in 2016. There was a table of four girls, just hanging out, having a good time. I went over to make sure they were happy with everything, and one of them gave me a napkin. As I opened it, she smiled.

"R U DTF US?" the words said on the napkin, scrawled in lipliner.

As someone who had suffered from insecurities and anxiety and who had regularly been mistaken as gay, finding out that these women wanted to bang me, it was hard to stay composed. I mean, I was no innocent; I had been around decadent sexual energy for years, working in bars and nightlife, but this was the first time it had been directed at me in quite such an assertive way. And by not one, but four beautiful women. This was some rock star shit, and my ego was absolutely loving it.

I knew I wasn't going to go home with them—I had never taken anyone home from work because I didn't want my staff to lose respect for me. But I did end up talking to them for a while, and I got one of their numbers—the girl who had written on the napkin. We ended up going on a date a few weeks later. Nothing serious came of it, but we remained in touch, as friends.

Then came New Year's Eve, and the girl I had briefly dated messaged me.

"Hey, me and the girls are hanging at Chateau Marmont for New Year's, wanna meet us?"

I went, we had a great evening together, and at the end of the night the girls went home to their respective apartments, and I went home to mine.

Next morning, I got a text.

"We're all hungover, want to have brunch?"

Well. It seemed as though they were enjoying my company. Feeling very happy about the way my life was unfolding, I met the four of them at a brunch spot, and after stuffing our faces, we went back to one of their apartments to watch a movie.

Everyone piled onto the couch, and within five minutes, one of the girls started kissing her friend. Before I knew it, all the girls were kissing each other. I sat there, frozen, not sure what to do. Should I leave?

One of them turned to me.

"Jeremy, aren't you going to join in? We thought you were a red-blooded man!"

All I knew is that I'd scrambled some eggs for dinner at Nighthawk, and now here I was, about to have sex with four gorgeous, super nice girls who for some reason wanted to start the new year by taking their clothes off with me.

For a moment, I felt slightly objectified, slightly taken advantage of, but that didn't last—before long, I was having a truly memorable afternoon, despite all the food in my belly. (We'd had a pizza cookie, a bazooka, for lunch. Actually, it was amazing that any of us were able to have intercourse after the amount of food we'd just consumed.)

We all remained friends for years, and I'll always look back on that New Year's very fondly. But times have changed. Or maybe I have, at least. For instance, I got a DM from a woman not so long ago, and it said,

I want you to cook me dinner . . . and breakfast . . . if you're man enough.

My first thought was *nope, never going to happen.* I'm not even sure she was a real person. Could have been a bot. Either way, no.

Next in my inbox was a DM from a guy who follows me and my podcast. I opened the message and it read,

Fat faggot.

I think my black nail gels had offended him.

And what was interesting about all of it—insults and flirtations, alike—is that it all seemed to take me back to the same place. A place in which my "masculinity" was being questioned.

"Am I gay?" I asked my mom once when I was eleven years old. In school, kids were always calling me "faggot," a horrible, abusive word, and it had happened so often that I'd started to wonder if maybe they were right. *Was* I gay, like Andy Warhol, and so many of my dad's heroes?

"Well, do you like any boys at school?" my mom said.

"I like my friends. They're okay, I guess."

"Do you like any girls?"

"Yes! I'm in love with all the girls in school."

"Then I don't think you're gay."

"Really?"

"Yes. Look, it doesn't matter if you like girls or boys, or both. Just finish your homework."

I moved on with my life, and by the time I became a teenager it was clear that my sexuality did, indeed, fall on the heterosexual side of the spectrum, even though my passion for moisturizer, clay masks, and alcohol-free deodorant fell very much outside macho "bro" culture. Either way, the playground bullies were wrong, as they always are, and I realized how lucky I was to grow up in a family where there isn't any stigma surrounding sexuality at all; where homosexuality isn't viewed as something to be ashamed of. Sometimes I actually wondered if my father, who still spent his days reminiscing about his glory days at the fabulous Studio 54, might actually have preferred that I had come out as gay.

Many years later, and several months into my therapy, I brought these incidents up with my Sarahpist. I was curious about masculinity, and whether my parents might have had some influence on the way I perceive it and myself.

"Jeremy, it's men's fathers who teach them how to be 'males' in the world, so I'm sure all this had a huge impact," she said.

"Did I mention, my dad gave me my first porn magazine when I was six?"

"No, you didn't."

"Yeah, Pamela Anderson was on the cover. Then he got me a *Hustler* and a *Penthouse*. I didn't know what sex or masturbation was, but when I looked at Pamela Anderson and the girls in the magazine, I knew I wanted to insert my thing inside them. I guess I lost my virginity early too."

"How early?"

"I was eleven. I mean, I was already six feet tall, so everyone thought I was older."

"Jeremy, your father set the blueprint for you on what being a man is all about. Let me ask you this—aside from a very open attitude towards sexuality, where did you and your dad connect, Jeremy?"

"Nightlife and music," I said immediately. "My mom was the food influence, but my dad was Limelight, Studio 54, Warhol, Basquiat. He would play the Rolling Stones, Pink Floyd, and Led Zeppelin for me, when I was six or seven years old. I knew what 'Stairway to Heaven' was years before any of the other kids in my class."

"So those were also the influences that shaped your perception of masculinity, and you've probably brought many of those ideas into adulthood," she said.

I thought about Mick Jagger and David Bowie. How they wore makeup, nail polish, and glitter and were incredibly feminine and lived generally heterosexual lives. All my dad's heroes were glam and nonbinary as fuck, come to think of it. Now it was starting to make sense—the nail polish, the confusion I felt regarding what it means to "be a man." It was because my dad, for better or worse, had imprinted a version of masculinity on me that didn't conform to mainstream society's version of masculinity at all.

Back to those black nail gels—I started getting them during the pandemic, and I kept up the manicures religiously. I usually just do black, and black matte for the holidays. But I do have my crazy ass nails, for special occasions, and I don't care what conclusions people draw from those choices. Brad Pitt has worn skinny dresses, Brad Pitt paints his nails, and Brad Pitt is the epitome of the stereotypically straight, good-looking guy. Who cares. When people think I'm gay or nonbinary or anything other than a heterosexual, male-identified person, I'm neutral on it. But I know it would bother a lot of my male friends.

Many males work very hard to project an image of masculinity. There remains, in my gender, a strong attachment to old, traditional ideas about what it means to be a man. These ideas remain entrenched, even as notions of masculinity are examined and reinvented, and even amid giant shifts in gender norms and power structures. Traits that are traditionally viewed as "masculine" in Western society—like strength, courage, independence, leadership, and assertiveness—no longer belong to men. They belong to everyone. And that's a good thing. But at the time of this writing, a bunch of dudes just decided to take away women's right to choose what to do with their own bodies, and all of a sudden it's clear that we haven't come very far at all.

Sometimes it feels like the main way men in my generation have been able to edge away from the old stereotypes has been superficial. We're way behind on developing empathy, but we sure have figured out how to consume more like women typically do.

My house smells like Aesop's, for instance. I insist upon high-quality shampoo. I host wine, cheese, and face mask nights with my girl friends, and I spend a LOT of money on Kiehl's hand lotion. Skin's the first line of defense against germs, bro; all men should have hand lotion. For years, American men were resistant to this kind of self-care, because it seemed counter to our programming, and now that's changing. Cool.

Still, despite our support of genderless beauty consumerism, despite our painted fingernails that cause trolls on the internet to DM us homophobic slurs—when it comes to truly taking ownership of our issues, the vast majority of us are still pretty much typical dudes.

FOR THE CULTURE

Rappers, I personally owe them a lot. As a man who had a complicated relationship with his father, I've created mentors and male role models for myself within the cultures that I appreciate, hip hop being a big one. From Pharrell, I learned to be open to evolution in all directions. From Jay-Z, I saw a blueprint of entrepreneurship, one in which artistry and business can function side by side. And despite the aggressive masculinity of the rap world, I've witnessed them lead the way in helping to break that paradigm down, and redefine masculinity in our culture in a way my other male idols never have. Rappers (and Harry Styles, also BTS) are dictating the future of masculinity, and taking it in a more interesting direction.

There's the surface stuff. For instance, the second A$AP Rocky started painting his nails, it became okay for everyone else to do it. When I started wearing skinny jeans, I had guy friends literally ask me if I was coming out of the closet—then Lil Wayne started wearing Vans and skinny jeans, and suddenly it was okay. Young Thug wore a dress on his album cover, and Lil Uzi Vert wore a woman's shirt because it was "cute." But the changes are occurring under the surface too.

Think about Tyler, the Creator's *Flower Boy*. Brockhampton's *Saturation II*. Music has always been about a communication of identity, and it's fascinating to see how hip hop artists have stopped adhering to the classic masculine mold of before and have begun to introduce more emotional features into their music. Because without emotions, how can you tell the whole story of who you are?

"I don't display emotions," 50 Cent once said. "I have every feeling that everyone else has, but I've developed ways to suppress them. Anger is one of my most comfortable feelings." Alpha behavior was always a way for Black males to assert their masculinity in a white society that persecuted and emasculated them. Style, power, and sexual confidence were everything, and you were a man if you were tough and intimidating. When rappers and hip hop artists expressed anything that might be considered feminine or homosexual, their whole identity as a hip hop artist came into question—until now. Until hip hop's shift from emotional concealment to expression got underway, and now it looks like there's no going back.

Many people think that rapper Kid Cudi's emotional honesty is what started changing rap forever. Cudi's breakout album, *Man on the Moon*, addressed his struggles with depression and anxiety, track after track. The honesty worked. The album drastically outsold expectations and people began to realize that vulnerability does not prevent success—it opens doorways to it. Ten years later, we heard Jay-Z saying he "gotta get softer," Tyler, the Creator telling listeners "you don't have to hide," and Frank Ocean confessing he fell in love with a guy who was "pretty like a girl." Instead of suffocating under rigid ideas of what it means to be a man, the rap world today is subverting all that, and it should be empowering us all to do the same.

"To change what it means to be a man, and be manly and masculine. That's why I said it's OK to get your feelings hurt, it's okay to admit that, and it's okay to cry because men can do that too," said Kevin Abstract of Brockhampton. With statements like these, rappers are laying the groundwork for a much more open and inclusive future for young men to step into, if we can find the courage to put aside our own egos.

That's the first step. For all of us, but especially men. We shouldn't hate ourselves for our flaws, but we should realize it's okay to talk about them, and get the help we need to be the strongest, healthiest versions of ourselves.

"If I ever see one of my male friends being toxic to his girlfriend, I will beat the fucking crap out of him," I heard some guy say once. He was trying, but it was embarrassing how much he missed the point. Men, we can keep talking about body image, self-acceptance, anti-blemish face masks, fluid sexuality, depression, manicures, more than ever before—but the real battle starts when we dismantle that pervasive and underlying assumption among us. The one that states that our worth relates to our ability to be rich, strong, fit, confident, virile, preferably with a giant dick. As we know, very few men check all, if any, of these boxes, and the result is shame, anger, and resentment, none of which we are supposed to express—except we usually do, in one way or another.

Society acts surprised when mass shootings occur, and glosses over the fact that they are almost exclusively carried out by young men.

Society acts surprised when men take their own lives at a much higher rate than the rest of the population—did you know men die by suicide 3.5 times more often than women?

Society forgets that it teaches men to pretend they're in control, even when we're not, resulting in levels of toxicity that the rest of the world has been choking on for a long time.

The masculine paradigm that encourages and excuses toxicity makes no real business sense. It's degrading and shameful, and only someone mentally ill can actually thrive in those kinds of environments. The next generation of male leaders, I hope, is starting to realize that.

Businesspeople, visionaries, public figures, artists, creatives—we're doing things differently, we're talking about our mental health, and we're questioning the correlation between masculinity and strength. Is there strength in the abuse of power? Or is it the weakest thing a man can actually do?

Or there's the alternative.

We can continue to pretend that our suppressed emotions and unhealed issues don't exist. We can put on one of our nine masks (have you read *The Mask of Masculinity* yet?) in our business, public, and creative lives, and perform the parts of the bullies and moneymakers and gangsters that society quietly pushes us to be. We can thoughtlessly adhere to the subliminal messaging of mainstream "masculinity," which pushes us towards inauthentic quests for power, wealth, and status at all costs.

We can paper over the damage we've done. We can issue half-hearted apologies and hire publicists to clean up messes. We can take short breaks before coming back and acting like nothing really bad happened. But what goes around comes around, and that's why successful men who have achieved the pinnacle of success are, fairly often, emotionally deficient human beings. They haven't gotten the help that they desperately need because they've never been trained to ask for it.

And all that darkness we've buried inside? We'll take that home with us at night. We'll numb it with drugs and alcohol. We'll unleash it on our family and romantic partners, because we've been trained to expect them to absorb the burden of our frustrations. Masculinity, the way we've designed it, is literally destroying lives, every fucking day. It's toxic, this idea of needing an external thing—whether it's an appendage, or a bank balance, or a car, or a career—in order to be happy. Following your dick will always lead you to inauthenticity and misery, if you let it. So let it go, guys. It's time to follow something else. As men, we have to trash the old ideas, ASAP, and come up with something new. Something that actually works.

9

LOOSE BALLOONS

Embracing That Willy Wonka Shit

O N MY LEFT FOREARM, I HAVE A TATTOO OF A BRAIN BEING LIFTED BY SEVEN BAL-
loons. A few centimeters away, there's an eighth. A loose balloon,
drifting off in its own direction, all by itself. No brain anchoring it to
the earth. No balloon buddies keeping it company. Just one loose balloon, breaking away, floating off in its own direction, and every time I
look at it, it reminds me to dream bigger. To push my ideas higher, no
matter how weird or "crazy" they might seem to anyone else.

You know what I mean by "crazy" ideas, right? The kind that make
people nod their heads and go, "Wow, that is so *interesting* . . ." The
kind that make zero sense on paper because they bubbled up from
somewhere deep in your subconscious, a rabbit hole that leads to a land
where nothing makes any logical sense. When I go down my rabbit

hole, what resides there isn't a Cheshire Cat, a super-stoned caterpillar, or some psychedelic mushrooms—it's a collection of those loose balloons, floating gently through the outer reaches of my imagination.

WTF IS A LOOSE BALLOON?

True creativity and artistry are born outside conventional notions of rational thought. Daydreams, night dreams, the poems we write when we're sad, the ideas we get while speeding along the freeway too fast during an anxious episode. We should never disregard these ideas, even if they aren't meant to be. They are beautiful because they exist. Sure, sometimes these ideas can make you money—why do you think so many entrepreneurs are microdosing every day? Because they WANT the loose balloons. Because you never know where they might take you. Sometimes they don't make you any money at all. But they're super important to have. And, in my opinion, they're absolutely vital to our mental health.

My brain is 65 percent creative, and 35 percent business. Meaning, I understand consumers, marketing, numbers, psychology, et cetera, but my mindset exists primarily outside the box. That's why people hire me, in the main. Because my mind can come up with innovative lightbulb ideas, as well as the tried-and-tested slam dunks. Take your pick. You want some chicken and biscuits? No? Okay, how about a restaurant where the customers create the menu the night they arrive? That would be interesting, right? Logistically, it would never work. But the fact that I allow myself to even have ideas like that indicates a baseline level of creativity that can be appealing, to some. It indicates "cutting-edge," "interesting," and even "groundbreaking," and even if they're not ideas anyone wishes to pursue to execution, just having them in the mix adds excitement to the creative process, and dimension to my own personal story and brand.

Think of loose balloons as concept albums. Take MF DOOM's *Mm . . Food*, where every track is inspired by culinary subject matter. I'm talking tracks like "Beef Rap," "Hoe Cakes," and "Rapp Snitch Knishes." Yes, it's an acquired taste, but it stands as living testament to the late rapper's ability to come up with a completely unexpected, experimental concept and make it work. Loose balloons can mean the difference between being known as good at what you do, and being fearless enough to dare to be groundbreaking.

What's Going On was the eleventh studio album by Marvin Gaye. Released on May 21, 1971, it was classified as R&B, but told a story from the point of view of a Vietnam veteran returning to his home country to witness hatred, suffering, and injustice, with themes of poverty and drug abuse, and even the ecosystem. Inspired by a protest song, and despite its raw, unflinching honesty, it was an immediate commercial and critical success.

R&B + The Story of an Imaginary Vietnam War Veteran = Sheer Brilliance, paper-clipped.

Loose balloons are for sure part of the paper-clipping mechanism. When you're in a loose balloon state, that's when you allow your mind to juxtapose things you'd never put together normally. Malcolm McLaren was an English artist, singer, songwriter, musician, clothes designer, and boutique owner, known for combining his talents and activities in utterly inventive ways, from managing the Sex Pistols to becoming a forefather of hip hop with his first album, *Duck Rock*, which spawned the pivotal singles "Buffalo Gals" and "Double Dutch" that introduced breakdancing, graffiti, and DJing from the Bronx to audiences around the world.

To be a monster paper-clipper like McLaren, you have to have an appreciation for the loose balloon, for "magnificent mistakes," as he called them, even with all the unpredictability they bring to the table. Likewise with the Studio 54 mentality in which you're faking it till you make it, creating your own personal fantasy using smoke and mirrors, and making it real. There's a mystical, intangible element to it that is a direct relative of loose balloon thinking. The kind of thinking that makes no sense and drifts into pure faith, even madness, at times.

The Rise and Fall of Ziggy Stardust and the Spiders from Mars by David Bowie is what made Bowie's fictional alter ego, Ziggy Stardust, famous. It was released in 1972 by RCA Records as a rock opera, and Bowie put together a story upon its release. It's about an androgynous, bisexual rock star called Ziggy Stardust who is sent to earth to save us from an impending apocalyptic disaster, and the character was supposedly influenced by English singer Vince Taylor, Norman Carl Odam (the so-called stardust cowboy), and Japanese fashion designer Kansai Yamamoto. Eventually, it became impossible for Bowie to separate Ziggy Stardust from his own offstage character. "My whole personality was affected. It became very dangerous. I really did have doubts about my sanity."

There's a creative dynamism that exists within the things we can't always control. Like mental illness. The rhythms of mania and depression, and it's well known that many artists are bipolar, to varying degrees. Look inside the mind of anyone struggling to manage their thoughts, and you may find a series of loose balloons, floating around. Sometimes, within them exist the seeds for ideas that might take you to the moon. The trick is catching them.

THAT WILLY WONKA SHIT

When you're ideating, try to allow space for a little insanity. Think of it as a mental exercise. Think of unworkable, impossible, borderline ridiculous ideas, and instead of completely dismissing them, write them down. Offer them space. Even the ideas that you know you'll never execute. Why? Because there's something deeply empowering about giving yourself permission to have impossible ideas. It helps keep the creative process fresh, fun, and boundless. It's healthy to let your imagination run wild. And ultimately, it doesn't matter if those ideas have any substance. It doesn't matter if they ever become reality. What's important is that they exist, out there, in the ether, as a reminder to always allow your mind to venture beyond boundaries and expectations. So when you feel a loose balloon floating up in your mind, let it fly free. See where it goes. Celebrate it for going to infinity and beyond, for venturing into space.

Cultivating creative freedom is easier said than done, and many people struggle with embracing loose balloon thinking, especially when they're trying to create on a commercial level, please a boss, or fit into a preestablished creative culture. Loose balloons don't always have a selling point, or a market, or a tangible reason for existence. A loose balloon may be born way ahead of its time.

Take the internet, for example. Talk about a loose balloon idea—until, of course, it evolved into an entire paradigm for modern humanity. Imagine someone in the 1950s pitching the idea of an invisible, wireless dimension that could govern the way people live, eat, shop, fall in love, and think, using computers. It would have been filed under science fiction, or developed into a storyline for *Star Trek*.

Think about Tesla—the man, not the car. Nikola Tesla (1856–1943) literally designed the alternating-current (AC) electric system, the predominant electrical system used around the world today. Everyone thought he was nuts, including his boss, Thomas Edison, who wound up making a fortune off electric light bulbs that ran on Tesla's AC electricity, while Tesla died penniless, mentally ill, and a laughingstock. Today, Tesla's inventions are considered the backbone of modern power, and the loose balloon of his genius is no longer overshadowed by the business success of Edison. But still.

As much as I advocate for loose balloon thinking, in practice I still struggle with it. My motto—"think outside the box, within a box"—betrays that, because the fact that I'm even acknowledging a box means I'm placing restrictions on my loose balloons. Even when I'm paper-clipping ideas and brainstorming like crazy, there are still certain parameters within which the ideas usually exist. That's because I'm an entrepreneur who exists in the world, not Willy Wonka hanging out with a bunch of Oompa Loompas in my chocolate factory.

On the days when a brainstorming session produces nothing but Willy Wonka shit, I might walk away feeling a little frustrated, like maybe I didn't accomplish enough. That's because of my programming that states ideas only have value if they serve a purpose, preferably one that makes money. We have to fight that urge to dismiss loose balloons, because if we're only creating while always thinking about a bottom line, we're preventing our minds from being truly free.

Cultivate a loose balloon mentality, and it will show you just how far your mind can really go. Even when you're creating to serve commercial needs, you'll have a sense of how far you could, in theory, stretch your vision. If you spend a lifetime limiting yourself, popping your loose balloons, and never allowing your mind to venture into uncharted territory, you'll never know what you're truly capable of.

Don't think about money.

Don't think about profit, or the bottom line.

Just start from a core of gut instinct, and allow yourself to play, at least once in a while.

That could mean creating outside your medium. If you're a musician, draw, sketch, create a film, cook—whatever the fuck you want to do—then feel free to throw all those ideas away. Watch them float off into space, on their own journey. Maybe they'll come back around again, when the time is right and the world is ready. Or maybe they'll disappear in the outer reaches of the galaxy, never to be seen again. It doesn't matter. All that matters is that they exist.

Loose balloon thinking is easiest when you're at the beginning of your career, or you've already achieved GOAT status and have more money than God, and can afford to have as many loose balloons as you want. Ideally, you want to be in that happy place where loose balloons and commercial viability are one and the same, where you can create at a high level with no limits, always, and where your career allows you to inhabit the true intersection of creativity and financial success.

But what if, like most of us, you're in that in-between space between newbie and deity? What if you're building something you really believe in, and it feels risky to be paying attention to loose balloons that could never support the house of cards? It might seem like the smart thing to do would be to reel in the balloons, for now. To pause outside-the-box thinking in favor of safe, tried-and-tested approaches.

Can you guess what I think about that? By this point in the book, you probably can.

I disagree.

When you're starting out, you might have more options in terms of where your imagination can go, because you have less to lose, and fewer people to please. But once you start gaining some level of commercial viability, you're going to do everything you can to hold on to that. And the tighter you hold on to old ideas, the less room they have to expand into something that can grow with the times.

Many of the world's greatest innovators were considered a little controversial when they were starting out.

Steve Jobs.

Warhol.

Van Gogh was never even recognized in his time.

What these innovators had in common was an unyielding commitment to their own vision. A loose balloon represents the most authentic version of yourself, a celebration of you doing you, in all your unique glory. Authenticity means you're not giving a fuck about what anyone thinks. Not worrying how other people are going to receive your ideas. Authentic creative ideation is the intellectual equivalent of dancing in your underwear when you're by yourself and nothing matters, because you don't care what you look like. You're busting out all your interpretive dance moves, most of which never see the light of day. Imagine doing that in front of people. Your moves are going to be different. You might put on some clothes. You're going to modify yourself, try to conform to what people think is cool and acceptable behavior.

But here's the paradox—while loose balloons may be the expression of our inner crazy, they also contain the keys to healing. All the things that made me feel anxious—a lack of authenticity, imposter syndrome, the need for external validation—have been most effectively treated by me doing the most authentic thing possible in that moment.

That means allowing yourself to just be you. To dance in your underwear, holding a bunch of loose balloons, reveling in the fact that you're alive and creating. Loose balloons are medicine, so long as we allow our minds to generate them, and set them free.

THE LOOSE BALLOON ALWAYS WINS

For years I was concerned about getting on medication, because I assumed that a stable mind was incapable of loose balloon thinking. Even though I was battling anxiety on a regular basis, along with a host of other troubling symptoms, I had come to rely on my manic creativity to a point where it was a part of my identity. I was terrified that medication would pop my loose balloons, or deflate them, and I wasn't willing to take the risk.

The truth is, I used to have more loose balloons, when I was younger. But that wasn't because I was unmedicated. It was because I was broke and possessed by the desire to stop being broke. It was because I had nothing to lose, no reputation, no responsibility to maintain a brand. Now, life is cool because I have resources, and people respect what I've done. People buy into my ideas because I have credibility in the creative space and have refined my execution, but I'm creating with a narrower lens. I'm not gonna call a big investor and pitch them a "dancing in my underwear" concept, because I know my limitations, from an execution standpoint. I know too much. I know how things are going to move in the market, how they might make an impact. Knowledge can be an enemy of loose balloon thinking. It makes it much harder to grab a blank canvas and tell myself, *do whatever the fuck you want.*

Medication turned out not to be the thing that created boundaries for me. What limited my creativity the most was, paradoxically, success. It's ironic, isn't it? You spend your whole life working towards something, and once you get it, it can cannibalize the very thing that got you there. Your creativity.

The more you feel a sense of responsibility to your legacy, and to keep your success going, the greater the inbuilt pressure to not be crazy with your ideas. To not innovate without boundaries. There's a reason why so many sophomore albums that follow amazing debut albums end up being really disappointing. When an artist establishes themselves within a musical genre, gains notoriety from it, and then wishes to move on but gets restrained by fan expectation and inertia. Sometimes it's because artists only have so many stories to tell, and they've crammed all their loose balloons into one product, without anything left over. So they're left to either draw from their old material or just rehash what they've already done. On top of that, the businesspeople around them may not want them to reinvent the script. Why create a new story when the older story did so well?

In people's eyes, I'm a successful Food Guy. But if I open a restaurant tomorrow and it bombs, that perception is going to change. I can't take that level of risk anymore. If I was just starting, who the fuck cares? If it doesn't work, it doesn't work. I can go through a hundred start-ups that don't work and it's not gonna really affect me, because nobody really cares. If you're successful and you fail, everyone will know.

The sophomore jinx applies to all industries—athletes' second season of play, TV show second seasons, and movie and video game sequels notoriously often fail to live up to the high standards of the first effort. You see this with actors all the time. "You're only as good as your last deal," they say, and we've all seen it happen. Actors who have a hit movie and are commanding millions of dollars per role, then all of a sudden they pick one bad movie and are forever tainted. Remember when *Star Wars Episodes II* and *III* ruined Hayden Christensen? The good news is, if and when that happens, there's usually one way to save the ship from sinking. Grab a loose balloon. Do an indie film that's risky but creative. Remember when Quentin Tarantino singlehandedly revived John Travolta's career with *Pulp Fiction*? At that point, an actor can jump between loose balloon indies to keep their career alive, and the blockbusters that keep their bank balances alive.

Shia LaBeouf was, in the early 2000s, considered Hollywood's next big thing. He got his start aged fourteen in the three-season run of Disney's *Even Stevens* and starred alongside Christy Carlson Romano for all sixty-five episodes of the series. From 2003 to 2006, LaBeouf launched a film career with *Holes*, *The Even Stevens Movie*, *Dumb and Dumberer: When Harry Met Lloyd*, *I, Robot*, *Constantine*, and *Disturbia*. In 2007, he was catapulted to stardom with his role in *Transformers* as Sam Witwicky. Then, thanks to his odd behaviors and legal troubles, he seemed to fade into the shadows, only returning in the form of bad news. *Indiana Jones and the Kingdom of the Crystal Skull* took him to the edge of disappearing for good. Remember in 2014, when he wore a brown paper bag on his head that read I AM NOT FAMOUS ANYMORE at the premiere of Lars von Trier's *Nymphomaniac*? But he began to make a comeback on the back of loose balloon projects, films like *Honey Boy*, *The Peanut Butter Falcon*, and *Pieces of a Woman*. Allegations of abuse from his ex FKA Twigs may completely undermine whatever brilliance exists there, though. Yes, he's developed a persona that exudes loose balloon creativity, but he's acknowledged that his past alcoholism and abusive behavior have hurt people. No matter how creative you are, your loose balloons will do you no good if you're battling mental health issues that harm others and send you on a path toward being canceled.

Let's discuss Nicolas Cage. Let's not forget he did fucking *National Treasure: Book of Secrets*. Absolute trash, in my opinion. Also his highest-grossing film, bringing in $457 million. It's his chicken and biscuits. Then there's *Mandy* and *Pig* and *Adaptation* and *Wild at Heart* and *Bad Lieutenant* and *Raising Arizona* and *Massive Talent* and a million other films that were critically acclaimed but grossed nowhere near as much in comparison. There's one story he's telling, though, and it runs throughout all his movies. And the story is that Nicolas Cage does whatever the fuck he wants. Those are the dots that connect in his narrative.

It's all about balance, in the end. Or having your cake and eating it, if all goes well. A balanced creative diet involves the basic carbs, protein, and fat, but also, every once in a while, a blue colloidal silver smoothie with every vitamin in it and crystals at the bottom. It's about having the chicken and biscuits, but having the loose balloons too. And even if you have a certain level of success, even when you're sure you can't afford to bomb, it's about never being frightened of those little balloons. Because they might just be the thing that saves you.

MOONSHOTS

Let's say tomorrow, I wanted to do something in the food space. And I wanted to be really creative. I would find a loose balloon, and present it as 100 percent art, a passion project, not as an actual project that I'm pushing out. Like a bizarre NFT—I'm not going to drop a collection of ten thousand, like I normally would; I'm going to drop a collection of ten. Or a weird pop-up in a tree in the middle of nowhere, and four people would be invited. Maybe a critic, an artist, a rapper, and my mom. All of whom would understand and appreciate the unique experience they were having. I wouldn't necessarily share it with the public at large, or a mainstream investor, because they'd think I had lost my mind.

Share your balloons with the right people. That's how you cover your bases. Don't present your loose balloon as your chicken and biscuits, your next big thing. Because there's a high probability it will fail miserably, in the context of making money. But treat those loose balloons as though they're intentionally not supposed to make money, and then it's a win-win. And it's a win-win-win if that loose balloon idea actually does go on to make money.

The Slinky, for example, was born after naval engineer Richard James created it by accident. He dropped a tension spring he was working with and watched it slink away across the floor. It took him two years of experimenting with different formulas to find the perfect slink-down-the-stairs toy he imagined in his head. Slinky is now in the National Toy Hall of Fame, with over 350 million sold and profits reaching $3 billion. He made a clumsy mistake, saw it as a loose balloon, and it made him a fortune. In 1960, he left his wife and family to move to Bolivia and join Wycliffe Bible Translators, which some call a Christian cult. Another loose balloon idea? Maybe. But nowhere near as successful as his Slinky.

Beanie Babies, created by Ty Warner in 1993, were the plush, bean-filled toy fad of the '90s. Warner's Ty Inc. reportedly made $700 million in one year, selling the Beanies for five dollars apiece. By 1999, the company had over $1 billion in sales. Warner made the decision not to sell the toys at nationwide chains like Toys "R" Us and Walmart, but instead driving up the market by selling them at small, independent stores and creating a craze. Some stores even received instructions from

Ty Inc. not to sell more than a certain amount to one customer. Beanies began going up on the resale market with five-figure asking prices.

The Chia Pet—clay figures filled with water and coated in seeds that sprout greenery—is a cultural icon. You can buy a Chia Pet version of a dog, cat, bunny, or even the president. The company sells five hundred thousand every holiday season. At sixteen dollars apiece, that means millions of dollars every year. The Mexican herb chia explodes with luscious springs of green when watered, and creator Joe Pedott credits the idea to his home in San Francisco and an agent at his ad firm's butcher of the name, ultimately leading to its infamous jingle "Ch-Ch-Ch-Chia!" that was heard for years on television commercials well into the 2010s. The toy was even included in a *New York Times* time capsule.

It's about finding that middle ground. If you go too far in either direction—commercial or conceptual—you're going to suffer. If you start dismissing your loose balloons, your shit's gonna get tired. *You're* gonna get tired, and bored, and actually that's really bad for your mental health. That's why people have midlife crises. The guy who's got it figured out, he's got the wife, the kids, the money, and everything that he was supposed to be working towards, but something is missing. And what's usually missing is the loose balloon, the ability to be creative, to be whimsical, to be wild and free and not give a fuck. He forgot how to do that so now he's buying sports cars and hairpieces, and just got the world's most cringe tattoo.

WHEN LOOSE BALLOONS FLY AWAY

Maybe you once liked your job and felt happy at home. But now you can't help but feel restless and apathetic. Maybe you've noticed that all the dreams you used to have remain unfulfilled. Or maybe you've accomplished so many career goals that you're left wondering if there's anything left to do. Boredom is the dark side of chicken and biscuits.

When this happens, chicken and biscuits–focused people work harder to create distractions for themselves. They're just postponing the inevitable, because when you feel unchallenged and unstimulated for long periods, it can take a serious toll on your happiness and relationships. It might make you think about moving to Bolivia to join a cult. It might make you splurge on a red Ferrari or rhinoplasty even though you have a mortgage to pay because you're filled with a sudden desire to *live life to its fullest,* and make up for all the things you let slip by in your youth. Or you might just fall into a deep depression, and not talk about it because it's "unmanly" to admit you feel down. Anxiety, I could tolerate it to a certain degree for several years, because there was an element of productivity. But the thing I always feared most was depression. Not being able to get out of bed, not being able to think creatively, not even having the ability to think outside the box or have a loose balloon if I tried. Depression is the least creative state. Depression is when we forget we ever had loose balloons to begin with.

Did you know suicide rates are highest among adults aged forty-five to fifty-four, according to the American Foundation for Suicide Prevention? The phrase "midlife crisis" definitely conjures up images of male indulgence and irresponsibility—a wealthy, middle-aged man who trades in the minivan for a pimped-out ride and gets a FUCK THE POLICE neck tattoo and starts having sex with women half his age— but before it became a gendered cliché, it actually was a feminist concept. Journalist Gail Sheehy used the term to describe a midlife period when *both* men and women might reassess their choices and seek a change in life. A midlife crisis isn't all about the clichés of buying sports cars and dumping your partner for a younger model. Gross. It's a moment when people become keenly aware of their mortality, reflect on their lives, and question what they can accomplish in the rest of their lives. It can have serious ramifications on your relationships, your career, and your mental health.

Sheehy's definition challenged the double standard of middle age—where aging is advantageous to men and detrimental to women—by viewing midlife as an opportunity rather than a crisis. The term was quickly appropriated by psychological and psychiatric experts and redefined as a male-centered, masculinist concept, but really, it applies to us all, whatever our gender. And I may not be an academic, but the root cause of these crises and resultant mental illnesses seems clear to me.

Too much chicken and biscuits, coupled with a distinct lack of loose balloons.

And the good news is, like all crises, a deficit of loose balloon thinking presents us with an opportunity to confront the question: Am I living the life I truly want to live? If you never properly addressed prior trauma in your past, these are the moments when it might come back into your mind. Now is the time to seek help, instead of just brushing those thoughts and feelings under the rug. These moments in life are an opportunity to refashion your life, turn off your autopilot, and be more deliberate about your decisions so you can become an even better version of yourself. Remember the things that made you happy when you had zero responsibilities. For me, it was making experimental sandwiches in my mom's kitchen at midnight. My first real loose balloons.

The loose balloon looks like an outlier, but it's our pathway towards the most important aspects of ourselves. A loose balloon is a thing to hold on to—not at the cost of your mental illness, but as a possible medicine for it. That was the biggest lesson for me—that you don't need to be mentally ill to cultivate and encourage your brain to adopt a loose balloon mindset.

Those little guys literally showed me the meaning of life. A possible shape for my future, where I could be happy and fulfilled and hungry forever. So when you're in a funk, or you're feeling like you need a jolt to get you out of a plateau, or you're wondering, *what the fuck do I do next?* That, my friend, is the time to wheel out your balloons. You might laugh at them now, but they could literally save your life.

10

FALLING UPWARDS

The Food Tastes Better When the Table's Not Wobbling

A FEW MONTHS AGO, MY SARAHPIST AND I DECIDED TO UP MY COCKTAIL OF MEDication to the highest dose possible. The anxiety was creeping back, and revisiting that state felt deeply uncomfortable, like being forced to spend time with a person I'd outgrown. When she suggested upping my milligrams, there was zero fear or hesitation on my part. Which is interesting, considering that eighteen months prior, I was completely against any form of medication, convinced it would rob me of all my creativity and burst my balloons. But the opposite happened. Because I was no longer battling the constant distraction of anxiety, my creativity actually went up. Which meant I was on board to do whatever it takes to maintain that state. Being on drugs—the right drugs—has been the best thing I ever did for myself, and if staying sane means upping my dosage for now, so be it. I'm in this for the long haul. Not just to feel good, but because it literally has elevated my business, and accelerated my career in ways I never thought possible.

How? I'll break it down.

I'm just as detail-oriented as my prior anxious self—but I don't suffer the spirals anymore, or sweat the small stuff.

I'm more confident—your confidence goes up when your anxiety goes down, and healthy confidence means you're usually more willing to just be yourself. When you're being yourself, it creates space for more authentic and fulfilling business relationships to flower. Win-win.

I have learned to see my imposter syndrome for what it is—a trauma response from growing up broke—and I've committed to authenticity in my public persona as a way to combat it. Another win-win, since a commitment to authenticity is what literally got me this book deal.

I still harness my good anxiety, like the power of broke—but since getting medicated, the good anxiety never pushes my thoughts into negative, spiraling doom zones. That's because my core is calm and uncluttered, and Alan, thank God, is no longer steering the ship.

Now, when I'm connecting dots in the bigger-picture through line of my career, it's along a more meaningful narrative, I think. My story is now about creating while pursuing authenticity and mental health, not just financial growth and status. I really prefer that.

Regardless of my nail polish and "femme" obsessions with bath products, I'm still a dude, albeit a dude who is paying close attention to his in-built tendencies toward toxic masculinity. Being in therapy really helped that, since it offered me a healthy outlet in which to vent my frustrations amid my ongoing pursuit of success, along with a structure for maintaining regular checks on my mental well-being. Too many men are still reluctant to ask for help or even admit they need it, and there's room for a whole new paradigm for how to be a dude in the world. It is possible for men to be strong, without suppressing our feelings and turning into toxic, shouty cock nozzles.

Post-treatment, my loose balloons are as present and inspiring as ever, especially now that I have the peace of mind to harness them in healthy and focused ways. Of course, I still feel that enormous pressure to put commercial needs above creative desires, but I always save space for those balloons. Without them, I'll stop enjoying what I do. And then what's the point? Then I'm on the road to a bad hairpiece and shitty neck tattoos at age fifty.

My anxiety cough, I am pleased to announce, is no longer an issue. It does pop up here and there, but it's manageable, and it usually goes away as quickly as it arrived. I literally cannot *wait* to go to The Brunch next Grammy season, and not bail suddenly because I'm about to cough my guts up all over the pasta bar.

Nonetheless, don't misconstrue this as some manifesto for world peace and universal mental health through medication. There's no such thing as a magic pill that will fix all our problems, or make us happy, successful, and fulfilled overnight. That's not how this works, alas. There are too many variables and surprises along the path to healing for me to lay claim to a panacea. I have no answers that offer global solutions. But I can tell you this with confidence—the combination of medication and therapy, for me, had such tangible benefits, it transformed me from being a passenger in a speeding car to the driver. There's no calmer mind than the one behind the wheel of a Formula One race car.

So as much as I hate recipes—seriously, fuck yo recipe—I can claim to have found a blueprint for creativity and happiness, for me. And it started with peace of mind. That was the magic ingredient.

RED LIGHT, GREEN LIGHT

One of the greatest tools I acquired in therapy was the traffic light system. Normally I fucking hate traffic lights. I find them deeply triggering and sources of anxiety. But the system I'm talking about exists in my head, and it's something my Sarahpist taught me to do in order to better handle my response to triggers.

In my days pre-treatment, whenever I felt anxiety, I experienced it from the inside out. There was no sense of separation. The spiraling thoughts became my reality, and I lived life on a dizzying, never-ending helter-skelter. Now, I've learned how to jump off the helter-skelter by activating my traffic lights. I've grown to love them, in fact. Who knew!

Here's how it works.

The red light is my anxious state. It represents the trigger that stops me in my tracks and causes my thoughts to spiral, shoving me straight into the anxiety vortex.

The yellow light is the in-between space, where I can decide whether to stay trapped in the tornado and let anxiety lead, or perform a thirty-second rewind that will eventually lead me into a green light space.

The green light is what indicates it's safe. I can separate myself from the trigger and move along with my day.

Let's say I'm having a moment with Bob, my imposter syndrome.

"Everyone here is richer and more beautiful than you. You'll never be as cool as them. You should just quit before they find out."

Instead of believing what that asshole is telling me in that moment, I press pause on his bullshit, take a breath, and step back. Zoom the hell out. Then, I try to identify what exactly is triggering me on the micro level to feel like an imposter in that moment.

"It's common for children of broken homes who grew up financially insecure, especially if they are people of color, to feel unworthy of success," I'll remind myself.

Over time, you begin to recognize the pattern in real time. It's that recognition and understanding that helps you step into a yellow light space.

"Oh, that's why I'm feeling like this. It's the same every time I'm at an exclusive event, or when I read mean comments online—my mind becomes vulnerable to Bob, and sometimes I let him lead me into a negative space."

As you start to identify those patterns, it becomes so much easier to break them.

Here are actual excerpts from my internal dialogue, whenever I'm triggered:

Red Light. STOP!

Why am I such a fake? I'll never fit in. One day they'll figure it out and my business will collapse and I'll lose all my money and wind up on the street near my mom's old café.

Wait—let's do a thirty-second rewind.

(Sound of tape rewinding.)

Flashing yellow: cross with caution.

Maybe I feel this way because I'm sitting at a dinner table with some people who are very successful. One of them just mentioned growing up in Beverly Hills and their Harvard degree. This is the information that caused me to feel unworthy.

But I've already had this feeling, many times, and this time, I'm prepared.

This feeling is rooted in the past, not my present, or my future.

This feeling is something I should try to let go of.

Green: safe to cross.

Check it out—the green light.

I'm ready to move on from this bullshit and continue to enjoy my life.

Therapy, combined with medication, enabled me to develop tools, techniques, and muscle memory, all of which help me stand up to Alan and Bob on a daily basis. Now, I understand why I'm feeling the way I do. And while the feelings won't always disappear immediately, they seem to have less power over me each time I encounter them. Less impact on the way I'm experiencing my life, because I am able to see the moments for what they really are: expressions of unhealthy internal thought patterns that I'm trying my hardest to break.

I have devoted space and time in my life toward understanding and treating my anxiety disorder. Before, I just let anxiety happen to me, and reacted whichever way seemed easiest. My mind would plunge into dark, chaotic places, and I'd have to battle to escape the panic by working more, driving faster, running away in circles, but always finding myself back at square one. I assumed my mind would eventually heal itself, somehow. That these patterns would fade away, instead of carving deeper and deeper grooves into my psyche. Grooves that were becoming scars. Scars that would bleed with every unhinged internal episode that I refused to talk about because I thought it was more important for me to *seem* okay, than to actually *be* okay.

Real talk: Writing this book has been kind of triggering. Mainly, it brought Bob back into the picture, and I really can't stand that guy. As I wrote, I'd hear him whisper in my ear, trolling my brain, like he always has.

I can't believe you're being published by one of the world's biggest publishing houses. Who fucking cares what you have to say?

Wait till they figure out they got the wrong guy—they clearly think you're someone else. Someone way cooler and more famous.

Having the opportunity to write this book was a dream come true, for me. And whenever Bob would show up while I was working on chapters, I had to remind myself that he was missing the point. I didn't get the opportunity to write a book because I was some kind of super-famous, iconic person. I'm not—I'm just a tall, anxious, Jewish kid with a lot of cool ideas. No, the reason I got a book deal was because I'm not perfect, and I'm kind of haunted by Bob, and Alan, and all those toxic assholes in my head. If I hadn't decided to open up about what's been going on in my head all these years, what the fuck else would I be writing about? No one, except maybe my mom, wants to read a list of Jeremy Fall's accomplishments. But they might want to read some writing from a guy in his early thirties who isn't super famous, or ultra-wealthy, but has figured out how to live his best life as a result of getting help and telling the truth.

That's it, Bob. Suck it up. The only reason I'm here is because I figured out how to get away from YOU.

THE ENJOYABLE ADULT THRILLS OF MENTAL STABILITY

So there's this record label I'm launching with Warner Music Group. In my opinion, it's one of the coolest goddamn paper clips I've ever come up with, if I do say so myself.

Picture this: a Web3, NFT record label.

Music + NFTs = The Paper Clip of My Fucking Dreams. Hello.

Let's take a moment to praise Jehovah, Buddha, and all known interdimensional deities for allowing this insanely beautiful loose balloon of an idea to even exist, let alone actually come to fruition. Which is it?

What we're developing looks like a traditional record label model, where you sign artists and put out their work, except we're going to release music-centric projects through the medium of NFTs. So simple, and yet, never been done. Kind of like a Breakfast for Dinner restaurant. Those are my favorite kind of ideas. They're so obvious, they kind of remain hidden in plain sight until people like you and me come along and decide to give them form. When we create out of thin air, we're making miracles. If that ain't some Old Testament, Book of Genesis goodness, I don't know what is.

Anyway—here's how this particular miracle is going to work. If an artist represented by our label releases a music video, for example, we will make it possible for their fans to own an NFT of each frame of said music video. Imagine owning one second of the video, or three seconds of the video, or more. Imagine owning a piece of Eminem's "Without Me" video, or Cardi B's "Bodak Yellow," or Dre's "Still D.R.E."? Not only would that be the coolest thing in the world, it literally unlocks a whole way for people to own valuable IP in the NFT space, while offering artists entire new revenue streams. It's a whole new ecosystem, and everyone's invited.

You may or may not give a flying flamingo about any of the above, NFTs, Web3, et cetera. But what you might find interesting, in the context of this book, is just how hardcore Bob tried to hack my thoughts while I was working on this idea. This was one of the biggest deals I've ever done, and he was super pissed.

Oh, now you're pretending like you're a record label dude? Of course! This reminds me of the time you pretended to be a chef when you're just a liar who eats Big Macs and fries.

I told you, Bob's the most toxic, unsupportive asshole in the world. He's the Freddy Krueger in my brain, and when he shows up, finger blades glistening, I know all my dreams are about to get eviscerated in his psychic bloodbath. But the thing is, it was actually so easy to ignore him, because no matter what he said, he didn't have a damn leg to stand on. Here's why.

The deal had all started in Twitter and DMs, when an executive at Warner noticed what I was doing in the NFT space and reached out to talk. Because my mind is hellbent on paper-clipping, it wasn't long before I saw ways to collaborate, and came up with the idea for an NFT label.

The convo went something like this:

"Yo, you wanna jump on a call? I have a cool idea."

(On the call.)

"Hey, what's up, Jeremy?"

"We should start a label."

"Oh, okay. Let me talk to my colleagues."

(On a later call.)

"Yeah. We like it. Like, so how do we do it?"

This entire glorious situation came about not from me talking my way into a room of suits, dripping sweat while pretending to be someone I'm not and trying to run PowerPoint so I achieve yet another goal that doesn't bring me anywhere closer to being happy, because Bob told me I don't deserve anything good. No, this happened through me being successful in the NFT space because that's where I feel most myself these days, which gave me the ability to talk to Warner Records and make something happen.

Imposter syndrome and Bob exist because we've established toxic metrics for "success." The younger Jeremy would probably have thought, *the day I'm able to make a deal with Warner Records, it'll be when I have ten million followers on Instagram and am a billionaire.* My stats do not fulfill the metrics my younger self latched onto, and without therapy and medication, I might have done this deal while wondering if I was, yet again, just an imposter in the space of success. It took therapy and medication for me to have the presence of mind to dismantle the old metrics and create new ones. The only metric for success I'm interested in now is the one where I'm doing things I really, truly believe in, because that's the real reward. That's the magic manifestation stuff that snowballs, that draws more good things in your direction. Bob has no idea what to do inside that paradigm. Bob kind of stands in the corner, trembling, scared to trip up on the through lines of authenticity that are crisscrossing his world, all of a sudden.

Bob, I'm doing me from now on, okay? And I'm happy to give you my Sarahpist's number, whenever you're ready.

EVOLUTION MARRIED THE MOGUL MENTALITY

Here's the part of the book where my mom gets to read her favorite paragraph.

Mom, this week, I did an art piece in collaboration with CNN. A few days before, I wrote a spoken word piece for a project I'm doing with Brandy, the iconic R&B musician. And I collaborated with the Notorious B.I.G. estate for a "Breakfast with Biggie" cooking video. Mom, I'm busy as hell, doing everything I've ever wanted to do, creatively, and I want to be able to keep doing that forever. Aren't you proud of me, Mom? Look, no hands!

It took me years to figure out that this is who I am. That I'm just someone who likes to create shit. That's it. That's my job description.

Creator of Cool Shit. Cool brands, cool concepts, cool experiences, with a big through line of food and music, and I'm constantly evolving, constantly exploring what that job description actually means.

In creative fields, we have to continually evolve. We have to stay hungry and engage with what's happening in real time. We have to keep questioning ourselves, who we are, what we stand for, and where we belong in a world that is constantly shifting. Otherwise, we're going to fall by the wayside. Just ask Tom from Myspace.

Evolution is the only way to survive in today's world, and it's really fucking hard to do. The inertia that exists when you've established your identity as a creative—that shit is real, and it's very easy to develop terror at the thought of doing something different and out of your wheelhouse, in case you fall flat on your face to the sound of Bob and Alan's shrieking, hyena laughter. But what's worse than that is to just keep fucking repeating yourself. Becoming pigeonholed into one thing.

I became known in my industry on the back of Breakfast for Dinner, and I would literally have lost all will to live if that was it. If that was all I was ever known for, and I became an old man sitting on a park bench talking about eggs after midnight to people who literally don't care. I had to step away from my Breakfast for Dinner identity, quick, before it took over. I had to force myself to evolve, because I didn't want every single subsequent project to be Breakfast for Dinner, with lipstick on.

It was hard, though, pulling away from the thing that put me on the map. Especially because I was still trapped in my anxious, unhealthy mind. Even for those who don't struggle with any mental illness, it's hard to break away from old ideas and evolve. There's a reason someone came up with "if it ain't broke, don't fix it." But that's not what I'm saying here. What I'm saying is, "if it ain't broke, walk away, and build something different."

Humans, on the whole, enjoy feeling safe and in control. But attachment to safety is dangerous in the creative fields. If you're playing it safe all the time, you're not giving yourself and your abilities enough credit. You *can* do better, and think differently, and first-time success doesn't have to be a one-time thing. Success isn't just a paper clip where A plus B equals C. Change it up! Pull out the B and make it a D. Flip it in different ways, scrap what you've done, and figure out how to make A + D = E. Keep doing that throughout your life, and you'll never be bored, and neither will the people around you.

You may have already experienced the external pressures to always do the same thing from the same angle. Do you know how many conversations I've had with investors, asking if I could just add Spiked Cereal Milk to the menu of a restaurant I'm designing that has nothing to do with Breakfast for Dinner?

Yes, Spiked Cereal Milk was a formula that worked. But it was just one dot in the story, so why retread our steps, people? Evolution means letting go. Not being beholden to the past, and being tuned in to the moment, to ourselves, and what's inspiring us. There are so many ways to take your ideas and let them grow into new, more interesting versions of themselves. You can expose them to different media, different ways of communication, different technologies, or even a stripping-away of technology. Never be scared to think along futuristic lines. Evolution and change are healthy, I truly believe that.

And for people like me, who grew up with financial insecurity and a certain doom and gloom about their future, evolution is literally our only hope for survival. In the beginning, I had a huge raging wildfire under my ass, telling me to get out of where I was, to escape myself and my perceived lack of worth, and become someone else. That definitely made it easier for me to evolve and take big leaps into the unknown. But it's not just courage and dreams and fear of poverty that allow us to evolve. It can also involve a lot of boring administrative tasks, or studying. Luckily, you can literally learn anything in the world on the University of YouTube, these days. The lines of communication are open between you and someone who can help you, thanks to the internet. There are gateways, all around us, if we're willing to search hard enough.

Because evolution doesn't just happen. It's based on the choices we make, and our willingness to face the things holding us back. Help is there for those of us struggling with mental health problems, or addiction, or low self-esteem, or bad relationships. But we have to choose it. That's the hardest part. My anxiety held me back. It fucked with me, but I was attached to it, even when all I felt was panic. Evolving beyond the walls I had built around my mind was one of the hardest things I ever did. I'm still working on it, day by day.

Okay. For all my talk of evolution and growth, there are definitely a few things that will probably never change about me. I am a creature of habit and I wear the exact same thing every day. It's black. There are twenty-five identical black T-shirts and ten identical black joggers in my closet. Another thing about me—I always watch comedy before I go to sleep, and I absolutely cannot watch sci-fi or fantasy—fuck *Lord of the Rings* and fuck *Harry Potter*. My brain operates way too fast for all that, and if confronted with magical realms full of trolls and wizards, it will literally short-circuit. Like, where do your dragons sleep, and what do you feed them? There's enough problem-solving humming through my mind at all times without me having to figure out the intricacies of domestic life in Middle Earth. So in that sense, I will probably never evolve.

What I do offer, though, is a blueprint for personal, emotional, spiritual, and business evolution, and the model that I espouse is very free-form. I would never want to advise you on how to make it in the food world or in nightlife or NFTs. But I am here as living proof that you can go on your own journey through many different creative spaces while constantly developing a clearer sense of who you really are, getting closer to that even as you're moving, evolving, and jumping in and out of different worlds rather than remaining confined to one.

We live in a time when there are no real set ideas on what a "career" looks like. It's okay to not be just one thing. You can be a dozen things, so long as you retain a core sense of who you are. That DNA will allow you to live like a mogul. You can be a billion different things and be a billion different people. You don't need to be trapped in who you think you are, or who you thought you wanted to be twenty years ago, or what other people think you should be, or what other people in your exact position are trying to do. None of that has anything to do with your journey.

HIGH VIEWS FROM AN ANXIOUS SIX-FOOT-SEVEN CREATIVE

My anxiety and I have a routine worked out. I still play out worst-case scenarios in my head. I allow my imagination to go wild with catastrophe. I let it happen and don't turn away, because the more I ignore my anxiety, the more it fights back.

Something about really getting to know Alan, and understanding what makes him tick, actually helped me become a better person. I understand my feelings now, and that has bled into everything I do. My relationships are better because I can communicate what's really going on. My thoughts are more innovative because I have grown my capacity to absorb information, without becoming overwhelmed.

The tightness in the chest, shallow breathing, clenched jaw muscles, frozen shoulders, gastrointestinal symptoms, skin breakouts, appetite changes, and radical shifts in energy—they're gone. The panic attacks that feel like heart failure are no more because I'm not stuck in negative thought loops that prevent me from moving forward, but keep me obsessing. Yes, it was possible that everyone I loved would die from the pandemic, but not probable. I became able to distinguish my worst fears from what was likely to happen, which finally gave me space to move forward.

I am an unreliable narrator, when I'm anxious.

But I will survive.

The future won't be what I thought, and that is a good thing, because it no longer contains catastrophic thoughts, self-judgments, and all-or-nothing ideas. I'm not over-scheduling, instead I'm focused on the work that really matters—and leaving time to take care of myself.

THE POWER OF NOW

I've been a little spoiled on my mental health journey, I think. A lot of it boils down to timing. When I started talking about mental health, it was in the post-COVID era, and stigma surrounding mental health was already beginning to fall away. When I went public with my mental health issues, I was essentially greeted with open arms, and I thank my lucky stars for that, every day. I can't imagine what it would have been like, talking about my problems to a hostile world. I mean, if I'd told stories about Bob and Alan and toxic masculinity in, say, the

1980s, the era of "greed is good" and "toxicity for the win," it's possible that my entire platform for "better business through mental health" would have fallen flat, or even worked against me. Let's be real: these are such recent changes, I might have been very poorly received as recently as five years ago.

But I was one of the lucky ones. I came of age at a time when space was already being made for mental health in the cultural conversation, and during the pandemic, society began to prioritize being honest about our inner struggles. As I became more honest, it reshaped the way I connected with everyone in my world. Being open about my issues made me more conscious of other people, and what they might be going through. Even my Sarahpist. I started to wonder how she was doing. A single mom running her practice and supporting her family . . . she was going through exactly what my mom had gone through. And with the world shut down because of COVID, I felt an overwhelming sense of concern for her.

One day, she had to reschedule a session because her seven-year-old daughter had gotten sick. We pushed the session back a few days, and when we finally spoke, I tried to offer my support.

"Sarah, is there anything I can do?"

"Well, you know, Jeremy, a therapy session isn't about me, right?"

"I know . . . but are you okay?"

"Jeremy, it's really important that you don't worry about me, or try to parent me. Those are old caretaking patterns we're moving away from. But is this hard for me? Yes. Do I feel isolated, much like you do? I do, Jeremy. It's a crazy time right now. I get it. But we're all in this together. This is a collective experience."

I have been able to pursue my own version of the American Dream. I came through some struggles and reframed my entire identity, at which point I realized that the American Dream forgot to teach us to be honest about our feelings and fears. My generation hasn't had many role models in that area, especially not among successful men. But we are starting to figure out that, actually, feelings and fears are what people want, because it's what we can all relate to. Not mad success and Hollywood lifestyles—who can relate to that unless you're obsessed and pathologically insecure like me, and started muscling your way onto red carpets at the age of sixteen?

We're facing a lot of darkness and chaos in the world—climate change, COVID-19 (which gave me the worst brain fog), but at least in one small way, things are getting better. It's okay to not be okay, anymore. You won't be judged in the way you might have been a few years ago. Superheroes don't really exist. The real superheroes are regular people, us, the ones who keep striving to be better, no matter what. It's okay to stumble on the path. It's okay to fall, because a lot of the time we're just falling upwards.

Depression and anxiety once had the potential to completely derail everything I had worked for in my life. But they also led me to make important decisions, not through choice but necessity. I made the decision to take care of my mental health and in doing so, I gave myself, and my ambitions, the greatest gift possible. That doesn't mean my life is perfect, or conforms to any of the stereotypes of what "success" is supposed to look like for young, ambitious men. But I'm proud to say that the last time I was depressed was more than two years ago, pre-medication. I've had down days, but never extended stretches. And the last time I felt my thoughts spiral, I had the tools to climb off of the helter-skelter, and walk away.

That, to me, is success.

Acknowledgments

To MY GHOSTRYDER, Caroline Ryder, for helping turn my insane stream of consciousness into words that make sense.

To my Sarahpist for keeping me in check when my thoughts didn't.

To Tess Callero and Clare Mao, my lit agents who reached out and believed I had a story to tell.

To my agents at WME—Misha, Zach, Chelsea, Haley, Jeff, Max, Molly, Sophia, Kate.

To the team at Hachette, thank you for giving me a megaphone to speak up about mental health.

To the ultimate OG—thank you, Lexapro. I don't know where I'd be without you (and gabapentin for my restless legs syndrome and late-night anxiety).

And for the record, we didn't kill him. It was the Romans.